Title Page

The Creative Awakening

Malcolm Dewey

Published by Malcolm Dewey, 2024.

Copyright

Dedication

To my children who will take their creativity into a new era.

Also to my wife for her support as we journey through our own creative awakening.

Life is a series of moments in the present. I look back at recordings from the past. The photos, the music. Nostalgia is a sweet drug that reminds me of my younger days. Happy moments lost forever. Yet I can feel those emotions. Does it mean I am reliving those moments? No, I can only live in the present. I have to remain in the present because I am alive and awake. I must create, make art, and celebrate life now. One day I can look back at this moment too and smile because I know I lived.

undefined

Why a Creative Awakening? Why Now?

" The state is not competent in artistic matters ... When the state leaves us free, it will have carried out its duty."

Gustave Courbet (1819-1877)

How much do you owe to your art? This may be a strange question for you. For most people I know, art does not figure into their lives that much. Why should they owe anything to art? I look at this another way. In our human development, art is fundamental to humanity and its success.

By art, I am referring to the human ability to work with abstract shapes and thoughts. An artist uses abstraction to create images and text, first in the mind in abstract terms and then into images, objects, and writing. Music, too. This breakthrough in humanity originated about 27,000 years ago, with cave paintings being the primary example.

Once humans could communicate big ideas using abstract shapes, sounds, and images, we accelerated in development. In a relative blink of an eye, we entered the Renaissance, the Industrial Revolution, and now the digital information age. These are big developments in humanity at high speed.

At a personal level, art has enabled me to live in a way that is true to my nature. I am a visually creative person at heart—I have been since I was a child. I have also worked as a professional in an office for twenty years, but that was not true to my nature.

When I was working an office-based career to make my way financially, I was disconnected from my passions. At an emotional level, I was getting by. But only just. Physically I would be stressed most of the time. This sometimes led to illness, poor sleep, and a "general malaise," as my doctor called it. I think he meant the human condition was getting to me, but most doctors focus on the symptoms, not the underlying condition. That is up to us to figure out. Something had to change, or a breakdown would happen. By returning to creativity and fine art, I am a much happier person. I am also helping and connecting with many more people who are on similar journeys. This book is an example of that connection. My paintings and painting tutorials are also examples of this connection.

It is at this personal level that I want to focus. The Creative Awakening is a necessary event within every person. Without this event, a person will remain disconnected from their true potential—the potential for living in the present, achieving a sense of purpose, caring, and sensitivity that exemplifies the human experience.

The next part of the question is, why now?

Of course, humans have had creative awakenings throughout history. The Renaissance is an example of this. It was a staggering period of evolving enlightenment that stretched over many generations. However, in modern times, these epochal shifts seem to happen quickly.

This century has seen massive events. One example is the September 11 attacks on the World Trade Centre. This event ushered in huge transformations in personal liberty, first in the United States and then worldwide. Not to mention the consequential wars that raged for over twenty years.

The other significant event was the 2008 economic crash. Some argue that this was the actual death of the Western monetary system, headed by the US Dollar. Ever since then, the world's reserve currency has been propped up with gargantuan money printing exercises on the back of various world-orchestrated crises. The result has been a devastating rate of inflation eating away at our plans for a "happy retirement."

Covid is another deeply divisive and disturbing example of a potential dystopian world. Then, there is war in the Ukraine and the Middle East. What is next? Another financial crisis, perhaps?

Is it any wonder that we mere individuals are reeling in confusion? Out of touch with our human need for security, creativity, and connection? As the quote above from Gustave Courbet illustrates, we need to be free from the state and its machinations to realize our artistic potential. Take it a step further and include freedom from corporate manipulations. Ultimately we need to free ourselves from our own limitations. Art, in its many facets, allows humans to live in the present. Mindfully and in peace. It is unlikely that we can change governments to a large degree. Instead, we creative people need to seek out what we can change. Focus on that by starting with our inner mindset.

In more rational, creative times, people could debate, express ideas, and have opposing views yet part ways amicably. No humiliation and social annihilation was contemplated for having differing views. Now, what is the position? Have we advanced social discourse, or have we reversed it? The latter must surely be the self-evident choice. What a sad state we are in.

I am not suggesting that we must take to the streets—not yet, and hopefully, it will never come to that. Freedom begins within yourself. If we are awake, we can see the manipulations, the bonds that bind our minds, and the media lies that keep us divided, fearful, and beholden to others for illusory security.

We can find creative awakening in our hearts and minds, in our homes. It is the ability to look to the age-old truths, to be self-aware, and to live in the now. In many ways, we see this with children before it is taught to them. They find joy and happiness in a moment. Creating is instinctive to a child.

I do take heart in the awakening already happening in the hearts and minds of many people worldwide. Personal health is an area that is seeing significant change. We are taking charge of what we eat, for example. The war on health has been growing since corporations fostered cereal-based diets and seed oils on humanity. This led to the outbreak of diabetes and obesity as the bane of Western health. Not butter, but Wheat! Refined wheat, sugar, and chemical-laden foods destroy a generation and threaten another generation. But the tide is turning, as they say. We are awake to corporate greed and the business that thrives off the chronically ill.

Then, how about the entertainment industry? Binge-watching junk on television. Celebrities peddling dystopian lifestyles. Materialism. Despite mainstream media's attempts to cover for the governments and corporations, all were revealed under the spotlight.

We want to be healthy again. Have a moral compass guiding our society. A return to common sense. A return to rational discourse. A return to art created by humans for the sake of enlightenment, positive expression, and belief in a higher purpose.

undefined

I want that freedom back—at least as close as I can get to it. That is what this book seeks to inspire: a creative awakening where each individual can find a clear compass reading on their creative direction without fear or interference from others. I envision a braver world with a return to values that our forebears struggled to secure for us.

The World Does Not Need More Artists

Have you heard the argument that the world needs more scientists, engineers, and technical people? Artists contribute nothing except pretty pictures.

I am sure you have encountered this argument. This view overlooks the vital role artists and creativity play in complementing science, engineering, and functional design. While disciplines like engineering and trades are crucial for providing practical solutions and essential services, art and aesthetics are what imbue our world with beauty, meaning, and soul.

Art, at its essence, is a journey into the human experience, a medium that stirs emotions and transforms the mundane into the extraordinary. While engineers and technicians construct the buildings we inhabit, it is the architects and designers who sculpt these structures into spaces that resonate with our souls. A lifeless concrete apartment block may serve its purpose, but a thoughtfully designed housing complex, infused with artistic elements, can metamorphose a living space into a sanctuary that nurtures our minds and spirits.

Art and creativity are not mere aesthetics; they are catalysts for innovation and problem-solving. Some of the world's most significant technological and scientific advancements have sprung from the fusion of technical prowess and artistic vision. The sleek, aerodynamic design of a Ferrari is not just about beauty; it is a testament to the union of engineering excellence and artistic ingenuity, resulting in a vehicle that is both high-performing and visually striking. Let's be honest. Unless that Ferrari is visually appealing, it doesn't matter how powerful the engine is. Car lovers crave speed and power but yearn to be captivated by its aesthetics as well.

In the realm of product design, the most successful and iconic creations are those that seamlessly blend functionality with aesthetic appeal. Apple's products, for instance, are not just highly capable devices but also beautifully crafted works of art that delight the senses and evoke emotional connections with their users.

Art and creativity also play crucial roles in areas like user experience design, where the ability to empathize with human needs and create intuitive, visually appealing interfaces can mean the difference between a frustrating and delightful experience for consumers.

Art can inspire and catalyze social change, challenge societal norms, and provoke important conversations. From powerful murals celebrating cultural heritage to thought-provoking installations that shed light on social injustices, art has the ability to transcend language barriers and connect with people on a deep, emotional level.

The differential in your Saab may be an engineering marvel, but it will not move you to tears like the Palchabel Canon in D Minor. Go on, I dare you to listen to the piece of music and not tear up.

While it is true that the world needs skilled engineers, technicians, and trades professionals to build and maintain our infrastructure, it is equally important to recognize the invaluable contributions of artists and creatives. Without their vision, our world would be a cold, soulless place devoid of beauty, emotion, and the spark of human ingenuity.

In an ideal society, we should aspire to strike a harmonious balance between the practical and the aesthetic, the functional and the inspiring. Engineers and artists, in a collaborative dance, should bring their unique strengths to the table, crafting solutions that not only function but also elevate the human experience. By embracing the synergy between art and science, we can forge a world that is not only technologically advanced but also profoundly enriched by the transformative power of creativity.

Art and Creativity are Not the Only Way

So far, I have argued that we need a creative awakening to free ourselves from dependence on the state and old cultural traps that keep us working up the corporate ladder and distracted by mindless activities. The counterargument goes more or less as follows: Personal happiness and fulfillment can be achieved through means other than art, and the significance of art in human development is overstated. In response to the counter-argument, several points can be made:

1. Multifaceted Paths to Fulfillment

Personal happiness and fulfillment are indeed multifaceted and can be achieved through various means, such as relationships, career success, physical health, and spiritual practices. However, this diversity of paths does not diminish the unique value that art and creativity bring to human life. Art offers a distinct way of engaging with the world that complements other avenues of fulfillment, enriching our emotional, intellectual, and spiritual experiences. I do believe that old ideas that keep people seeking external validation, rewards, and acknowledgment are designed to keep us weak and distracted, beholden to other power structures.

2. Unique Contributions of Art and Creativity

Art and creativity contribute to personal and societal well-being in ways that are distinct from other activities. Through artistic expression, individuals can explore and convey complex emotions, foster empathy, and gain deeper self-awareness. Creative activities also stimulate critical thinking and problem-solving skills, which are valuable in all areas of life. Art can bridge cultural and social divides, promoting community understanding and unity.

3. Historical and Cultural Evidence

Historically, art has played a crucial role in human development. From ancient cave paintings to contemporary digital art, creative expression has been fundamental to human culture and communication. Art captures and preserves cultural heritage, influences social change, and allows people to reflect on and make sense of their experiences. Some said that creativity would be smothered by modern technology. We would stop reading and simply remain blobs on the sofa watching re-hashed sequels on television. Yet, we are reading more now than ever. Creativity is open to many more people, but we must take the next step and get to work.

4. Psychological and Neurological Benefits

Numerous studies have shown that engaging in creative activities has significant psychological and neurological benefits. Art can reduce stress, improve mental health, and enhance cognitive function. For example, art therapy is used to help individuals cope with trauma, anxiety, and depression. The act of creating art can trigger the release of dopamine, a neurotransmitter associated with feelings of pleasure and reward.

5. Enhancing Quality of Life

Art enriches our lives by bringing beauty, joy, and meaning. It provides a means of escape and reflection, offering a break from the routine and the opportunity to see the world from different perspectives. Engaging with art—whether as a creator or an appreciator—can lead to moments of profound insight and connection that might be less accessible through other activities. Remember that those in positions of authority trying to keep us divided and in an agitated state fear humanity coming together through creativity. A common appreciation for art, creativity, and the sharing of ideas empowers people.

6. Interconnectedness of Creative and Non-Creative Pursuits

Creative thinking benefits many non-artistic pursuits. For instance, innovation in science and technology often involves a high degree of creativity. Encouraging creative expression can lead to breakthroughs in various fields, demonstrating that art and creativity are integral to broader human progress.

While personal happiness and fulfillment can indeed be achieved through various means, the unique contributions of art and creativity to individual and societal well-being are significant and multifaceted. Art enhances life's emotional, cognitive, and social dimensions, fostering a deeper awakening that complements other sources of fulfillment. By valuing and integrating art and creativity into our lives, we can achieve a richer, more balanced experience of happiness and fulfillment.

The Importance of Creativity in the Digital Age

"Art is to console those who are broken by life." Vincent van Gogh

undefined

Let's focus on our current state of living. In this modern age, the overwhelming presence of technology has had a profound impact on our sense of well-being. The constant exposure to mass media, smartphones, and binge-watching has created a constant stream of information and entertainment that demands our attention and can lead to a range of negative effects.

The 24/7 news cycle bombards us with sensationalized stories that evoke fear, anxiety, and stress, ultimately distorting our worldview.

Smartphones have become an integral part of our lives, offering an endless array of apps, social media platforms, and notifications that constantly vie for our attention, leading to decreased focus, productivity, and increased stress levels.

How often do you see people holding conversations while peeking at their phones? This technology promises to keep us all "connected," but not in a way that brings us together. Sadly, this lack of community is the norm these days.

Binge-watching television disrupts healthy sleep patterns, decreases physical activity, and contributes to a sedentary lifestyle. The addictive nature of binge-watching also leads to a sense of disconnection from reality and decreased social interactions.

These technological influences diminish our overall well-being by contributing to heightened levels of stress, anxiety, social isolation, and a decreased sense of fulfillment in our daily lives.

Recognizing these impacts is crucial. We need more mindful engagement with each other and moments of peace with ourselves.

The digital world offers numerous distractions that hinder our ability to connect with ourselves and engage in creative pursuits. Social media platforms capture and hold our attention with endless scrolling feeds, notifications, and curated content, consuming valuable hours that could be dedicated to exploring artistic endeavors.

Online entertainment, such as streaming services and online gaming, easily lures individuals into extended periods of passive consumption, leaving little room for creative expression. Digital distractions, like constant connectivity through smartphones, disrupt our focus and make it challenging to engage in deep, uninterrupted creative work.

The vast amount of online information can be overwhelming, leading to analysis paralysis or information fatigue. Instant gratification through likes, comments, and shares creates a mindset where pursuing long-term creative projects takes a backseat. Instant gratification is not how we further our lives.

While valuable resources, online courses, and tutorials can become a form of procrastination or a substitute for hands-on practice. Constant exposure to flawless art online can lead to self-doubt, imposter syndrome, and discouragement, deterring individuals from pursuing their artistic passions. I always encourage doing over simply consuming. The former is life-enhancing. The latter is only entertainment.

Recognizing these distractions, establishing boundaries, and engaging mindfully with technology is crucial to creating space for creativity, art, and personal growth.

Art provides a respite from the digital world and helps us reconnect with our true selves in several ways.

Engaging in art requires focused attention and mindful presence in the present moment. It allows us to detach from digital distractions and reconnect with our inner thoughts, emotions, and creative instincts. Art provides a medium for self-expression without the filters and limitations often imposed by the digital world, allowing us to communicate our ideas, perspectives, and emotions in a raw and authentic manner.

When last did you sit down with a blank piece of paper, paints, pencils, or whatever you prefer, and simply create a picture? Does something like this seem unattainable? Frivolous, boring, or a waste of time? Unrealistic on a busy day? Yes, for too many, this simple creative pleasure is set aside for being busy. I know that the time I spend painting is some of the most enriching and meditative time I can have. It may be only forty minutes, but the impact on my feel-good state of mind is huge. Maybe I can share that process with my art friends, and the effect will be multiplied. It is like magic. A super-power of sorts.

Art has a therapeutic effect on our emotional well-being, offering a safe and cathartic outlet for processing and releasing emotions that may be suppressed or overlooked in the digital hustle and bustle. Creating art engages our senses in a profound way, grounding us in the physical world and providing a stark contrast to the intangible nature of the digital.

Creativity helped me overcome stress and pressure in a busy law firm, reconnecting me with my family through the medium of art. Teaching my children to paint during their school years made art an important part of their adult lives. Two of my sons paint, and the third is a writer. Without a connection to my creative nature, I may have been upset by my children's artistic ambitions. Thankfully, I know that there is potential for emotional and material wealth in these creative careers. Importantly, I know that my children will have a well-rounded life experience and a deeper sense of fulfillment.

Speaking of "the youth of today," millennials are losing enthusiasm for the future. Relationships between humans and the sexes are at an all-time low. This troubling viewpoint was raised by Eric Weinstein, a mathematician and brilliant philosopher. How will this impact populations, ideas, and development for the future? Not very well, to say the least. Look up his podcast, The Portal, for more thoughts on the modern social construct.

Individuals can take practical steps to break free from the digital world's distractions and embrace creativity. Setting boundaries for digital media consumption, creating a dedicated creative space, and scheduling specific blocks of time for creative pursuits. Planning intentional breaks from digital devices through digital detoxes or designated screen-free days allows individuals to recharge and refocus on their artistic endeavors. Embracing mindfulness techniques (more on this later), prioritizing offline activities, joining creative communities, setting creative goals, and reflecting on the benefits of creativity all contribute to breaking away from digital distractions and fostering a healthier and more balanced relationship with technology.

Mindful Creation: The Power of Art in the Creative Awakening

"Art is the proper task of life. " Friedrich Nietzsche

undefined

In the fast pace of modern life, where chaos often takes center stage, the profound link between mindfulness and the initiation of a creative art journey emerges as a guiding beacon in pursuing a Creative Awakening. Will we take steps towards **cultivating mindfulness** and **embarking on a creative venture?** When these two ideas meet, there is transformative potential.

Mindfulness as the Gateway

Mindfulness is the practice of being fully present and engaged in the current moment. It serves as the gateway to unlocking our creative work. In a world saturated with distractions, mindfulness provides a sanctuary—a mental space where the incessant noise fades and our thoughts do not harass us. It is in this mindful space that art is created.

The Art of Being Present

Starting a creative art journey necessitates **a deliberate act** of being present. We make the decision to change our lifestyle one small step at a time. Whether wielding a paintbrush, strumming a guitar, or shaping words on a page, the act of creation demands our full attention.

Mindfulness enables us to shed the burdens of the past and future, allowing us to immerse ourselves in the current act of creation. This is meditation with action, a practice that I personally find easier to achieve and more rewarding than traditional meditation techniques. Perhaps this is because of my Western lifestyle and Type A personality. What is important is that it works.

The act of creation demands my undivided attention. I also get to create something with my hands, which gives me a physical measure of my time—a practical result I crave outside of the digital realm.

Creativity as a Meditative Process

The creative process becomes a form of meditation—a practice that transports individuals into a flow state. The mind enters a meditative rhythm as colors blend on a canvas or melodies intertwine in a composition. In this state, stress dissipates, and the mind's relentless chatter fades away. Creating art becomes a therapeutic journey, a pathway to self-discovery, and a means of attaining inner balance.

Mindful Exploration of the Self

Engaging in a creative art form becomes a vessel for a mindful exploration of the self. Through art, we can process our emotions, thoughts, and aspirations. This introspective journey, guided by mindfulness, unveils layers of self-awareness, fostering personal growth and a deeper connection with one's authentic identity. Does this sound too esoteric? If you are new to these ideas and practices, you may be skeptical, but at least try them. Practitioners of meditation and psychology have long advocated that we try to step away from our thoughts. Those distracting and damaging thoughts give anxiety. They will step away and observe the thoughts, not engage them, but simply let those thoughts pass on. When last did you choose not to be triggered by something and simply let the offensive thoughts, words, or events pass you? In essence, those thoughts are not offensive. It is our reaction to them that is important. Do we give those thoughts life, or do we let them float away?

Breaking the Chains of Perfection

Mindfulness liberates the creative spirit by breaking the chains of perfection. The incessant pursuit of flawlessness often stifles artistic expression. However, through mindfulness, we accept imperfections as integral parts of the creative process. Art becomes a journey of self-expression rather than a destination of perfection, encouraging risk-taking and an absence of self-reproach.

A Creative Awakening Through Mindful Living

Through mindfulness and creative expression, a profound Creative Awakening emerges. This awakening is not merely about creating art for art's sake; it's about living mindfully, embracing the beauty of the creative process, and realizing the potential for transformation that lies within every artistic endeavor. Through mindfulness, we discover that the act of creation is not just a means of expression; it is a pathway to inner freedom, self-discovery, and a life rich with purpose.

Overcoming Fear and Finding Confidence

Fear and self-doubt, these common obstacles, can be transformed into stepping stones that lead to the full embrace of creativity. These fears, which can manifest in various ways, such as the fear of failure, perfectionism, self-criticism, lack of time, comparison and judgment, fear of vulnerability, lack of support, and external pressures, are not insurmountable. Acknowledging and challenging these fears can unlock your creative potential and allow you to express yourself authentically.

Embarking on the journey to overcome these barriers necessitates the cultivation of self-awareness. It's about identifying the specific fears and excuses that are holding you back. By challenging negative beliefs and embracing a growth mindset, you can shift your perspective. Instead of seeking perfection, you can focus on learning and progress. Starting small and breaking down larger creative projects into manageable tasks can help build momentum and confidence. Embracing imperfection and practicing self-compassion are not just helpful, they are essential in nurturing a positive mindset and overcoming self-doubt.

Don't just consider seeking support from like-minded individuals and joining creative communities as a suggestion. It's a crucial step in your creative journey. These communities provide more than just encouragement and inspiration. They offer constructive feedback that can help you grow. Setting realistic goals, making time for creativity, and prioritizing the creative process over external validation is crucial in fostering a sense of fulfillment and personal satisfaction. You can confidently push through your fears and engage in creative activities by practicing courage and taking action.

Self-confidence is not just a factor, it's a vital role player in embracing creativity. It provides the belief in one's abilities and the courage to express oneself authentically. Cultivating self-confidence is not a one-time task. It's a continuous process that requires acknowledging and celebrating past achievements, practicing self-compassion, embracing failure as a learning opportunity, surrounding oneself with supportive individuals, taking small steps and celebrating progress, challenging comfort zones, seeking constructive feedback, practicing self-belief and positive affirmations, emphasizing the joy and process of creating, and persisting in the face of self-doubt.

Personal stories and examples of individuals who have conquered their fears and gained confidence in their artistic pursuits are potent reminders of the transformative power of embracing creativity. Artists such as Vincent van Gogh, Frida Kahlo, Georgia O'Keeffe, Jean-Michel Basquiat, and Yayoi Kusama have all experienced personal insecurities and setbacks but persisted in becoming influential figures in the art world. Their stories inspire and demonstrate the importance of self-belief, resilience, and the willingness to take risks.

In addition to these famous examples, many artists have taken personal risks to pursue their artistic passions. Whether giving up a stable job or closing a successful practice, these individuals demonstrate the bravery and determination to follow their creative dreams. The key is not recklessness but the willingness to take calculated risks and step outside one's comfort zone.

You can employ various strategies and exercises to build confidence and embrace the joy of creating. Starting with small, achievable goals, practicing regularly, embracing the process rather than fixating on the outcome, experimenting with different mediums and styles, seeking constructive feedback, celebrating milestones and achievements, surrounding oneself with supportive peers, engaging in creative challenges, documenting and reflecting on the creative journey, and practicing self-compassion are all practical approaches.

By implementing these strategies, you can gradually build your confidence, find joy in the creative process, and embrace the fulfillment of expressing your unique artistic voice. The journey to overcoming fear and finding confidence in creativity is ongoing. Still, with perseverance and self-belief, you can unlock your creative potential and experience the transformative power of embracing your creativity.

The Transformative Power of Art

In times of difficulty and turmoil, art can be a powerful tool for individuals to cope and find solace. It offers a unique avenue for emotional expression, catharsis, and healing. Engaging in art demands focus and concentration, leading to mindfulness that provides temporary respite from overwhelming thoughts and worries. Art also offers a sense of control and empowerment, allowing individuals to regain agency over their circumstances. Through the creative process, art has the potential to transform adversity into strength and resilience. It fosters connections and builds supportive communities, providing comfort and encouragement. You can explore and construct personal narratives with art, finding meaning and self-discovery. Critically, art can inspire and uplift, evoking feelings of awe, wonder, and hope even amid challenging circumstances. By embracing art, individuals can tap into its therapeutic qualities and find solace, emotional release, and personal growth. Throughout history, numerous artists have recognized and articulated the transformative power of art in their lives. Pablo Picasso once said, "Art washes away from the soul the dust of everyday life." Frida Kahlo found solace, healing, and self-expression through her art, stating, "I paint self-portraits because I am so often alone because I am the person I know best."

Vincent van Gogh believed that art brought meaning and purpose to life, stating, "I am seeking. I am striving. I am in it with all my heart."

Let us take a closer look at how Vincent van Gogh's art served as a powerful outlet and means of coping with the immense emotional turmoil and trauma he experienced throughout his life. His challenging childhood, marked by domestic upheaval, poverty, and a strained relationship with his parents, left deep psychological scars. Later in life, van Gogh grappled with what was likely bipolar disorder or another severe mental illness, enduring bouts of depression, psychosis, and mania.

Through his art, van Gogh found a way to channel his intense emotions, inner torment, and heightened sensitivity onto the canvas. His brushwork became increasingly expressive and agitated, with swirling patterns and bold, unmixed colors conveying a sense of feverish energy and passion. Art historians have noted how his style shifted during periods of psychological crisis, with his works becoming more turbulent and emotionally raw.

The time van Gogh spent in the asylum at Saint-Rémy in 1889-1890 proved one of his most prolific periods. Confined but with a modest studio, he painted many of his most iconic works, including The Starry Night, Irises, and Wheatfield with Crows. These paintings are renowned for their vibrant, swirling compositions and highly symbolic, almost hallucinatory quality that scholars believe reflected van Gogh's fragile mental state.

So, while van Gogh's mental illness brought him tremendous anguish, his artistic expression allowed him to transcend his suffering, if only temporarily. His paintings gave visceral, unrestrained form to his inner psychological landscape. In this sense, art was both an expressive outlet and a means of self-preservation for the tormented genius. The intense emotion and passion poured into his works have immortalized van Gogh as one of the most brilliantly creative artistic forces in overcoming personal trauma through the cathartic process of artistic creation.

Georgia O'Keeffe found that art enabled her to communicate and express emotions and experiences beyond words, saying, "I found I could say things with color and shapes that I couldn't say any other way - things I had no words for."

Salvador Dalí viewed art as a means of accessing the subconscious and expanding the boundaries of reality, famously stating, "Give me two hours a day of activity, and I'll take the other twenty-two in dreams."

These artists, among many others, have recognized and experienced the profound impact that art can have on self-expression, healing, and personal growth. Art has transformed human life in numerous ways, positively impacting individuals, communities, and society. It provides personal expression and empowerment, allowing individuals to find their voice, gain a sense of identity, and cultivate self-confidence. Engaging in art can positively impact emotional and mental well-being, providing a cathartic outlet for processing emotions, reducing stress, and promoting self-reflection.

Art serves as a vessel for preserving and celebrating cultural heritage, fostering a sense of belonging, pride, and cultural continuity. It brings people together, fostering social connections and building communities. Art education is vital in developing critical thinking, creativity, and problem-solving skills. Sadly, there is little of this curriculum available in schools anymore. I recall my art theory lessons with fondness. Our teacher was unconventional and sometimes grumpy, but he loved the subject, and we learned so much about life while studying art through the ages.

Art can evoke empathy and foster understanding by providing a window into diverse perspectives and experiences. Public art initiatives can transform urban spaces, rejuvenate communities, and foster civic pride. Art has catalyzed social and political movements, inspiring conversations and driving social change. The transformative power of art is not just a concept; it's a reality that we can all be a part of, and that's something to be hopeful about. Does all this seem too pie-in-the-sky for everyday life? It's not. To experience the transformative effects of art, you can incorporate it into your daily life in practical ways. Engaging in creative activities, cultivating an art collection, exploring art appreciation, starting an art journal, participating in art challenges or prompts, creating a visual diary, incorporating art in daily rituals, and sharing and collaborating with others are all ways to embrace art and tap into its transformative power. Individuals can enhance self-expression, personal growth, and overall well-being by prioritizing art and creating space for creative activities, appreciation, and reflection. The most important practical step? Start with what you have right now. You have the power to transform your life through art. Art possesses a transformative power that can bring solace, healing, and personal growth. It allows individuals to express complex emotions, find release, and regain control. Art has the potential to transform adversity into strength and resilience, foster connections, and build supportive communities. It enables individuals to explore personal narratives, find meaning, and engage in self-discovery. Art inspires and uplifts, evoking a sense of awe, wonder, and hope. By incorporating art into your daily life, you can tap into its therapeutic qualities and experience its transformative effects. No wonder the world would be better if art assumed more prominence in our lives.

Art is for the Rich and Leisured

The notion that art is solely for the wealthy and privileged is a misconception that fails to recognize the profound impact and accessibility of artistic expression across all socioeconomic strata. While it's true that the art world often caters to those with disposable income and leisure time, the transformative power of creativity transcends financial barriers. It offers a path for the economically disadvantaged to find solace, self-expression, and even economic mobility.

Art, throughout history, has not only been a medium for marginalized communities to voice their struggles and celebrate their resilience, but also a catalyst for social change. From the vibrant street art that adorns urban landscapes to the rich traditions of folk art and craft, artistic expression has emerged as a means of resistance, empowerment, and cultural preservation for those living in poverty or oppression.

The act of creating art is not just a form of self-expression, but a potent form of therapy. It provides an outlet for individuals to process their emotions, find meaning, and cultivate a sense of purpose amidst challenging circumstances. For those facing economic hardship, the simple act of drawing, painting, or crafting can serve as a source of solace, a reprieve from the daily struggles of poverty, and a means of nurturing one's mental and emotional well-being.

It's essential to recognize that art is not limited to the conventional forms found in galleries or museums. Art can manifest in the most humble of materials and spaces, from the intricate patterns woven into baskets or textiles to the intricate murals adorning the walls of underprivileged neighborhoods. These expressions of creativity beautify their surroundings and instill a sense of pride and cultural identity within the community.

Art also serves as a pathway to economic empowerment for impoverished people. Craft-based arts, such as pottery, woodworking, or jewelry-making, provide opportunities for individuals to develop marketable skills and generate income by selling their creations. Organizations and initiatives that support and promote these artistic endeavors can play a crucial role in empowering economically disadvantaged communities and fostering sustainable livelihoods. This fact is amply demonstrated in my home country of South Africa. I still recall the wonder of seeing clay horses crafted by young artists in rural areas of the Eastern Cape. These kids would run alongside our car, holding the clay horses to the window. My dad stopped the car so that we could take a closer look. Each horse was made from brown river clay and decorated with white paint. The bristles were used to create the horse's mane and tail. Of course, we had to buy a few of these artworks. I was utterly captivated. The kids put some money in their pockets and were happy, too.

This is a tiny example of creativity from financially poor rural areas. Many examples of artists making a very good living despite their beginnings in poverty-stricken circumstances. The accessibility of art and creativity is indeed its biggest strength. Talent will always come out of hiding if given an opportunity.

It's also worth noting that access to artistic experiences and education should be viewed as a fundamental human right rather than a luxury reserved for the privileged few. By incorporating art education into schools and community centers, we can nurture creativity, self-expression, and critical thinking skills in children and youth from all socioeconomic backgrounds, opening doors to personal growth and future opportunities.

Art is not a privilege but a fundamental human need, a means of self-expression, cultural preservation, and personal empowerment that transcends economic barriers. Rather than dismissing art as a pursuit for the wealthy, we should embrace its transformative potential and ensure that creative outlets are accessible to all, regardless of financial circumstances. By fostering a Creative Awakening that celebrates the universal language of art, we can uplift marginalized communities, cultivate empathy and understanding, and create a more equitable and enriching society for all. This is something to keep in mind when looking at how your local community allocates funding. Not to mention governments. Those that make provision for the arts are making a difference.

Rediscovering Your Inner Creative Spirit

Unleashing Your Creative Potential

Have you lost your artist's mojo? Perhaps you created once in another lifetime, but life got in the way. Your creative spirit has been buried for a long time. Is there any hope of restoring it? In this chapter, we will explore the process of rediscovering your inner creative spirit. What common blocks can hinder creativity, and what strategies will overcome them? By recognizing and addressing these obstacles, you can tap into your innate artistic abilities, reignite your creativity, and cultivate a fulfilling creative practice. Self-Doubt and Fear of Failure: The first block we will address is self-doubt and fear of failure. Many artists question their abilities and fear making mistakes, which hinders their creative expression. To overcome this block, it is essential to practice self-compassion and remind yourself that making mistakes is a natural part of the learning process. Embrace the joy of creating rather than seeking perfection, and focus on your growth and progress. As I always say, there is no art police. Making "mistakes" is not a crime nor a social faux pas. In truth, making a mess while creating art is one of the few remaining freedoms left in this crazy world. Go for it! Perfectionism: Another common block to creativity is perfectionism. The relentless pursuing perfection can stifle creativity and prevent individuals from taking risks. To overcome this block, embracing imperfections and allowing yourself to make mistakes is important. Give yourself permission to take risks and experiment, emphasizing the process and the learning experience rather than solely focusing on the end result. Forget Instagram and the fake stuff we see there. Make art and work with the messy process along the way. Nothing is perfect. Those fake photos of perfection are illusions. Not real life at all. We are all just humans trying to get through the day. Who knows the trials and tribulations each of those strangers is going through? What counts is showing up in your studio, at your desk, or wherever you do your thing and getting the job done. That is the win. Procrastination: Procrastination is a common block that prevents creative projects from taking shape. Breaking tasks into smaller, manageable steps, setting deadlines, establishing a routine, and creating a supportive environment that minimizes distractions can help overcome this block. Taking proactive steps to combat procrastination can create the space and time needed for your creative pursuits. Believe me, unless you get honest with yourself and cut the bull.... you will not get your art done. Procrastination takes many forms, and you can rationalize it in a million ways. The truth is that it is killing your creative life. Be aware. Be strong and kick the procrastination habit. Lack of Inspiration or Ideas: Feeling stuck or lacking inspiration is another block that individuals often encounter. To overcome this block, expose yourself to new experiences, explore different art forms or mediums, and seek inspiration from nature, books, music, or art exhibitions. Engage in activities that stimulate your imagination and spark new ideas. By immersing yourself in the world of creativity, you can reignite your inspiration and find new avenues for artistic expression. Put your feet up with a good art book. Let the ideas and creative juices bubble. Then start something while these ideas are fresh in your mind. **Information Overload**: Too much information or choices can overwhelm the creative process. Setting boundaries, limiting information intake, and simplifying your approach is important to overcome this block. Focus on one idea or project at a time, allowing yourself to dive deep into it. By simplifying and streamlining your creative process, you can alleviate overwhelm and foster a sense of clarity and focus. In short, stop scrolling through social media and start making something with your hands. **Comparison and Self-Criticism**: Constantly comparing oneself to others can stifle creativity and lead to self-criticism. Overcoming this block requires cultivating self-awareness and focusing on your unique voice and perspective. Celebrate your own progress and growth rather than comparing yourself to others. Remember that creativity is a personal journey, and each individual's artistic expression is unique and valuable. Your own art is wonderful. Keep making it. **Lack of Time**: Busy schedules can make finding time for creative pursuits challenging. Overcoming this block requires prioritizing creativity, scheduling dedicated creative time, and making it a non-negotiable part of your routine. Even short bursts of creativity can be valuable. This is an important point. Sometimes, I put in forty minutes of painting in a day. Yet that intensive flow state produces my best work. This is a powerful tip. You can nourish your creative spirit by carving out a little time for your creative practice. Even create your next masterpiece. **External Judgment and Criticism**: Fear is a huge problem. The fear of judgment and criticism from others can hinder creative expression. Overcoming this block involves surrounding yourself with supportive individuals, seeking constructive feedback from trusted sources, and reminding yourself that creativity is a personal journey. It is not solely about external validation but about the joy and fulfillment of self-expression. You are stronger than you believe. Create despite the fear. Your confidence will grow, but there will be setbacks too. Sometimes, work does not turn out as hoped. The next one will be better. This is how the process goes, so you may as well make friends with it. As an example, I can mention the unpleasant social media trolls I have had in the past. I have received comments on my art, my YouTube videos, and social media that would make a sailor gasp. These comments are very few and far between, but they do stand out at the time. Block, delete, and move on. I feel sorry for these rotten souls. I hope they find their light one day. **Routine and Monotony**: A monotonous or rigid routine can stifle creativity. To overcome this block, it is important to introduce variety and spontaneity into your routine. Explore new environments, try different techniques or styles, and intentionally seek out opportunities to break from the familiar. You can infuse your creative practice with freshness and vitality by embracing novelty and the unknown. In short, have some fun. **Lack of Confidence**: A lack of confidence can hold individuals back from fully expressing their creativity. To overcome this block, it is important to set achievable goals, practice regularly, seek positive reinforcement, and remind yourself of past successes and the transformative power of art. By building confidence in your abilities, you can unleash your creative potential and embrace your unique artistic expression. By recognizing these blocks to creativity and taking steps to overcome them, you can unleash your creative potential, embrace your unique artistic expression, and cultivate a fulfilling creative practice. Remember that creativity is a journey, and each step you take towards rediscovering your inner creative spirit brings you closer to a more vibrant and fulfilling life. Embrace the challenges, celebrate the victories, and let your creativity soar. I have faith in you.

Mindfulness and Art: A Perfect Pairing

Art has long been recognized as a powerful means of self-expression and a source of beauty and inspiration. Similarly, mindfulness has gained popularity as a practice that cultivates presence, awareness, and inner peace. The connection between mindfulness and artistic expression is profound and mutually beneficial. In this chapter, we will explore how mindfulness and art can enhance the creative process and bring about a sense of inner peace. At its core, mindfulness involves being fully present in the current moment and cultivating awareness of one's thoughts, feelings, and sensory experiences. This state of presence is also essential to artistic expression. When artists engage in their creative work, they often enter a state of deep engagement and focus, where they become fully absorbed in the act of creation. This immersion allows them to experience each brushstroke, word, or note with heightened awareness and presence. Have you experienced this? Maybe you have but did not realize you were enjoying a mindful moment of flow-state painting. You know that you had a wonderfully relaxing time painting. You finished your painting and felt calm, happy, and at peace. That was what the psychologists call a mindful experience.

Personally, this is how I meditate. I am not great at traditional meditation. I would rather have a nap if I am going to remain perfectly still for thirty minutes. I much prefer to merge into a flow state of mindful painting. Mixing color. Moving the brush and making brushstrokes is a profound way of calming your mind. This flow state brings a sense of calm, timelessness, and peace. The mindful awareness of the present moment that art encourages also fosters a sense of tranquility and connection with the artwork. Mindfulness encourages keen observation of the present moment without judgment. Artists who practice mindfulness develop a heightened sense of observation, enabling them to notice subtle details, nuances, and inspirations in their surroundings. This deepened observation informs their artistic choices and enriches their creative work as they see and appreciate the world with greater depth and clarity. This is a powerful idea. When I speak about "seeing like an artist," I usually mean the ability to see the subject in its composite parts. Light and shadow shapes.

Color notes. Also, to see potential compositions out of scenes that are boringly normal to non-artists. When you can focus on the nuances, you can translate that awareness into shapes of color on your canvas. It is a painting superpower! One key benefit of mindfulness in the artistic process is the enhancement of creativity and flow. Mindfulness can cultivate a state of flow where artists experience a sense of effortless concentration and a seamless, joyful process of creation. In this state, ideas flow naturally, and you become fully immersed in the creative act. The result is a heightened sense of creativity and a deep connection to the artistic process. Emotional awareness and expression are also enhanced through mindfulness. By practicing mindfulness, artists develop emotional intelligence, allowing them to authentically access and express their emotions. This ability to tap into their inner experiences enables artists to channel their feelings into their work, producing art that communicates depth and authenticity. You may start seeing other people overreacting to silly things. People get triggered by social media while driving or constantly gossiping about so-and-so. These negative things are distractions from your heightened awareness. You are more in control of your emotions and would instead remain in a peaceful state of mind. Of course, you will have moments of falling back into old habits. We are human. Fortunately, you will note these lapses and become more resolved to stay on the path of mindful living, letting the bad moods go by. More often than not, you will see the bad mood coming, prepare yourself, and see it on its way in short order. Do not languish in a negative mood for any significant length of time. Mindfulness also encourages non-judgmental exploration. Through mindfulness, artists can free themselves from self-criticism, perfectionism, and fear of failure. This attitude of non-judgment allows artists to explore and experiment with creative ideas without the pressure of meeting external expectations. It enables greater creative freedom and risk-taking, creating innovative and unique artistic expressions. See how this idea of mindfulness connects to the many creative blocks we discussed earlier? Heightened awareness of self is the key to freedom from all these blocks to your creative joy. Self-reflection and insight are powerful benefits of incorporating mindfulness into the artistic process. Mindfulness practice fosters self-reflection and introspection, allowing you to better understand your artistic intentions, motivations, and creative methods. This self-awareness enhances artistic decision-making, facilitates growth, and helps you to align your creative expression with your authentic self. Self-acceptance is a beautiful thing. Art allows individuals to express and release emotions, thoughts, and experiences. Artists can channel their inner world onto the canvas or paper through creative expression, allowing for emotional release and catharsis. This process brings a sense of relief, clarity, and inner peace. Engaging in artistic expression offers an opportunity for self-exploration and reflection. As artists create, they delve into their thoughts, memories, and perceptions, gaining insights into their inner landscape. This reflective process can lead to self-discovery, self-acceptance, and a deeper connection with oneself, fostering inner peace. Art can evoke a sense of transcendence and beauty, stirring emotions and inspiring awe. The experience of encountering or creating something visually or emotionally captivating can transport individuals beyond their immediate concerns and into a state of wonder and peace. This encounter with beauty can bring a sense of harmony, serenity, and inner stillness. Art can also remind us of the impermanence of life and the fleeting nature of experiences. Creating or appreciating art can cultivate an acceptance of impermanence, helping individuals let go of attachment to outcomes and embrace the present moment. This awareness of impermanence fosters a sense of peace, aligning with existence's transient nature. This state makes us more grateful for our lives, our loved ones and the bliss of being able to create art. Life is short and fragile. We must be grateful for the opportunity to appreciate art and participate in the creative process. Completing an artistic creation or achieving a personal goal can bring a sense of accomplishment and fulfillment. This sense of achievement contributes to inner peace by instilling a feeling of purpose, satisfaction, and personal growth. It is another opportunity for gratitude. We can employ various techniques to incorporate mindfulness into the creative process. Setting an intention to approach the creative activity with mindfulness is a powerful starting point. Engaging the senses by noticing the texture of materials, the sound of brushstrokes, and the colors and forms being worked with can anchor us in the present moment and deepen our connection with the creative experience. Slowing down, pausing, and observing the creative process without judgment are essential. Cultivating a beginner's mind, letting go of preconceived notions, and approaching the activity with fresh eyes and curiosity can enhance the mindfulness experience. Staying present with the breath as an anchor to the present moment can help maintain focus and attention. This reminds me of the importance of breathing correctly. All too often, we breathe too shallow. Breathing in the upper chest instead of breathing low into the core of our body. Your stomach should move in and out. Use this technique if your painting session starts to get tense. Your mind may be wandering into old negative thought loops. Be aware of this, pause, and take deeper breaths. Resume your work when you are back at the center. Embracing imperfections and practicing self-acceptance are crucial aspects of mindfulness in the creative process. Letting go of the pressure for perfection and embracing the authenticity and uniqueness of the creative process can bring about a sense of peace and self-compassion. Personal experiences of how mindfulness has enhanced artistic expression vary from individual to individual. For some, breaking a train of thought and regaining a centered state of mind through physical exercise can pave the way for a more mindful creative experience. Engaging with music and preparing materials can help me get into the mood for creating. These personal experiences highlight the importance of finding what works best for yourself in incorporating mindfulness into the creative process. Overall, mindfulness enhances the artistic experience and the outcome in several ways. It heightens focus and attention, improving concentration and a deeper connection to the creative task. It facilitates a flow state, where artists experience heightened creativity and a loss of self-consciousness. Mindfulness also increases awareness of choices, promoting intentional decision-making that aligns with the artist's vision. It encourages authentic expression, emotional regulation, and resilience, leading to a more balanced and composed approach to art. Finally, mindfulness fosters a sense of fulfillment and well-being, bringing joy, satisfaction, and purpose to the artistic journey.

Finding Inspiration in Nature

Nature has long been recognized for its healing and rejuvenating power, with cultures embracing its profound effects on well-being throughout history. The stress reduction offered by spending time in natural environments, such as forests, parks, or by the sea, is well-documented. Nature provides a respite from the demands and stimuli of daily life, allowing individuals to unwind and find calm. Nature has a restorative effect on mental well-being, alleviating symptoms of anxiety, depression, and mental fatigue. It offers an opportunity to disconnect from the pressures of modern life and reconnect with the simplicity and beauty of the natural world.

The Japanese have an excellent practice called forest bathing. Also known as "shinrin-yoku," it refers to immersing oneself in nature, particularly in forested areas, to promote physical and mental well-being. The Japanese have developed this idea with certified forest therapy guides who lead individuals or small groups through specially designated "therapy trails" in forested areas. These guided walks encourage participants to engage all their senses, practice mindfulness exercises, and connect with the healing properties of nature. But beyond its healing qualities, nature also serves as a wellspring of inspiration for artists. Artists from various disciplines can tap into the abundant inspiration that nature provides. By spending time in natural settings, observing and studying the intricate details, patterns, colors, and textures found in plants, landscapes, or natural phenomena, artists can capture the essence of nature in their creative work. Nature can influence your artistic creations' tone, color palette, and overall mood. Nature can contribute to finding inner peace and mindfulness. Engaging with nature encourages artists to be fully present in the moment, fostering mindful awareness. Nature provides a sanctuary from daily life's mental clutter and noise, allowing the mind to quiet down and enter a state of mental clarity. Several renowned artists serve as examples to illustrate the power of nature as a source of inspiration. Claude Monet, a leading figure of Impressionism, found great inspiration in nature. His famous series of water lilies, haystacks, and Rouen Cathedral paintings were all inspired by his observations of the changing light, colors, and reflections in nature. Georgia

O'Keeffe, known for her large-scale flower paintings and dramatic landscapes, found profound inspiration in nature. She often explored the southwestern United States, drawing inspiration from the expansive desert landscapes, vibrant flowers, and bones of animal skulls. Andy Goldsworthy, a renowned environmental artist, creates sculptures and installations using natural materials in their specific environments. He works directly with nature, creating temporary pieces influenced by the landscapes, seasons, and materials he encounters. Ansel Adams, famous for his black-and-white landscape photography, found inspiration in the grandeur and beauty of nature. His iconic photographs depict natural landscapes' power, serenity, and intricacy, showcasing his deep connection with the environment. Katsushika Hokusai, a Japanese ukiyo-e artist, drew immense inspiration from nature, particularly Mount Fuji. His iconic woodblock print series, "Thirty-Six Views of Mount Fuji," captures the mountain's beauty, scale, and spiritual significance in Japanese culture. Bringing nature into your artistic process is not just a theoretical concept, but a practical and accessible approach. You can take your sketchbooks, canvases, or art materials outdoors and create directly from nature, capturing the textures, colors, and forms that inspire you. Nature walks and gatherings can provide opportunities to explore different environments, observe and gather natural materials, and bring them back to the studio as references or collage elements. Nature photography can capture the beauty and details of nature, serving as inspiration for future artworks. Incorporating natural materials and found objects into artwork can add an organic and tactile quality, connecting it directly to nature. By using nature-inspired color palettes, you can infuse your work with the beauty of the natural world. These practical steps will not only stimulate more ideas but also enhance your creative output over time as you explore these ideas further.

I do not want you to feel overwhelmed with these suggestions. Not everything can be done right away. Some of these excursions into nature may not be possible without some planning around your busy life. Others may be simpler to achieve, like a walk near sunset to observe the light in your part of town. By observing nature, you will see much more and be inspired, too. By immersing themselves in nature's beauty, energy, and inspiration, you can develop deeper connections, meaning, and profound insights. Nature is a constant reminder of our interdependence with the natural world, the passing of time, and life cycles. The journey of artistic expression intertwined with nature is profound, offering a path to self-discovery, connection, and creative awakening.

The Joy of Creating: Embracing the Process

There exists a profound shift that can elevate the creative experience from a mere means to an end to a transformative journey of self-discovery and fulfillment. This shift lies in the act of the process rather than fixating solely on the result. By shifting our focus to the process, we unlock a world of joy, growth, and mindfulness that enriches our artistic practice and nourishes our souls. First, embracing the process allows us to fully immerse ourselves in the present moment and derive pure enjoyment from the act of creating. By relinquishing our attachment to the outcome, we free ourselves from the shackles of outcome-oriented thinking and instead revel in the sheer delight of the artistic process itself. The process-oriented approach fosters a spirit of exploration and growth. By embracing the process, we permit ourselves to experiment, take risks, and explore new ideas. We release the fear of failure and view mistakes and setbacks as valuable learning opportunities. In this way, the process becomes a continuous journey of discovery and personal and artistic growth. Artistic authenticity and personal expression are also helpful when we focus on the process. By shifting our focus away from external expectations and societal pressures, we can tap into our authentic selves and express our unique perspectives through art. The process becomes a space for self-exploration, experimentation, and the freedom to create without judgment. Our art becomes a genuine and meaningful reflection of who we are. The process also cultivates mindfulness and presence in our creative practice. We become fully engaged with our materials, techniques, and ideas when we focus on the process. We bring our attention to the present moment, immersing ourselves in the tactile sensations and sensory experiences of creating. The act of creating becomes a form of meditation, a conduit for mindfulness, and a deeper connection with our artwork. This idea is a powerful antidote to the pressures of perfectionism. By shifting our focus away from the result, we release ourselves from the burden of achieving a specific outcome. We learn to embrace imperfections, take risks, and enjoy the journey. The process becomes a sanctuary where we can celebrate imperfections and find beauty in the unexpected. Cultivating a sense of playfulness and curiosity is essential for unlocking our creative potential. By infusing our artistic process with playfulness, we can break free from limitations, explore new possibilities, and invigorate our creative practice with joy and curiosity. To do so, we must adopt a playful mindset. We must let go of the pressure to create something perfect or meaningful and permit ourselves to enjoy the process of experimenting, exploring, and having fun. Shifting our mindset creates a space for uninhibited creativity and opens ourselves to new artistic horizons. Experimentation is another critical strategy for cultivating playfulness and curiosity. We invite novelty and excitement into our artistic practice by stepping out of our comfort zones and trying new materials, techniques, or mediums. We embrace the opportunity to learn something new and approach it with a spirit of curiosity, allowing ourselves to be surprised by the unexpected outcomes that arise. Engaging in creative prompts and challenges is another avenue for cultivating playfulness and curiosity. By participating in prompts or challenges, we are encouraged to think outside the box, explore new ideas, and push the boundaries of our creativity. These prompts inspire fresh approaches, ignite our imagination, and stimulate our curiosity, leading to playful and innovative artistic outcomes. Incorporating elements of surprise is yet another strategy for cultivating playfulness and curiosity. We invite unexpected outcomes and fresh perspectives by introducing elements of randomness or chance into our artistic process. Whether randomly selecting colors, using unconventional materials, or incorporating chance-based techniques, embracing the unexpected can lead to playful and inspired artistic results. Collaboration with others can also foster playfulness and curiosity. We invite new ideas, techniques, and perspectives into our creative process by engaging in art exchanges, group projects, or partnerships with fellow artists. This collaboration opens us up to new possibilities, sparks our curiosity, and gently takes us out of our comfort zone. This is one way we can grow as artists. Taking breaks and exploring other sources of inspiration is a strategy that can invigorate our artistic practice with playfulness and curiosity. By stepping away from our artwork and immersing ourselves in different art forms, cultural experiences, or natural environments, we feed our curiosity and spark new ideas. These breaks allow us to recharge, gain fresh perspectives, and infuse our art with renewed playfulness and curiosity. By embracing a "What if?" mindset, we foster a sense of playfulness and curiosity in our artistic practice. By challenging assumptions, experimenting with unconventional ideas, and letting our imagination run wild, we open ourselves up to new and unexplored artistic territories. This mindset encourages us to think outside the box and approach our art with wonder and curiosity. In artistic pursuits, countless individuals have found joy in creating. Artists such as Wassily Kandinsky, Henri Matisse, Yayoi Kusama, Keith Haring, and Romero Britto epitomize this joy. Wassily Kandinsky, a pioneer of abstract art, infused his paintings with vibrant colors, dynamic forms, and energetic brushwork, reflecting his inner joy and passion for creative expression—a connection with folk art traditions and a child-like playfulness and whimsy. Henri Matisse, known for his vibrant colors, playful shapes, and sense of spontaneity, embraced bold experimentation and celebrated the lightness and joyousness of the creative process. Matisse kept on working despite age and infirmity. Through her immersive and whimsical installations, Yayoi Kusama invites viewers to immerse themselves in her imaginative and playful world, infusing her art with a sense of joy, wonder, and infinite possibilities. Keith Haring's iconic, bold, and energetic artwork embodies joy, spontaneity, and social activism. It spreads messages of love, unity, and joy to a wider audience. Romero Britto's colorful and vibrant art radiates joy and optimism. It celebrates life and encourages viewers to embrace happiness. These artists inspire us by reminding us of the profound joy that can be found in the artistic process. Their art embodies playfulness, exuberance, and a celebration of life, inviting us to embrace the joy of creative expression. Focusing on the process rather than solely on the end result has a multitude of benefits. By embracing the process, we engage in mindful exploration, freeing ourselves to experiment, take risks, and discover new possibilities. We release ourselves from the pressures of perfectionism, allowing our authentic selves to shine through. The process becomes a sanctuary for creativity, growth, and self-expression. The process-oriented approach fosters flow—heightened focus, productivity, and enjoyment. Time seems to fade away in this state, and we experience a sense of effortless creative energy. The process becomes a conduit for mindfulness, presence, and a deeper connection with our artwork. Focusing on the process enriches our artistic experience, promotes personal and artistic growth, and fosters a deeper connection with our creative practice. By embracing the joy of creating and infusing our artistic process with playfulness and curiosity, we unlock our true creative potential and embark on a transformative journey of self-discovery and fulfillment.

Giving Back with Genrosity

Cultivating a spirit of spontaneous generosity and considering the well-being of others is an essential aspect of the journey toward creative awakening. While pursuing personal growth and creative expression is essential, it should not be a solitary endeavor. By including acts of kindness, appreciation, and compassion towards others, you enrich the lives of those around you and deepen your sense of connection and fulfillment.

Here are some ways we can incorporate moments of generosity into our creative awakening journey:

1. Practice random acts of kindness: Seek opportunities to brighten someone's day through small, unexpected acts of kindness. It could be as simple as paying for the person behind you in the coffee line, leaving an encouraging note for a stranger, or offering to help someone carry their groceries. These little gestures can have a profound impact and spread ripples of positivity.

2. Share your talents and skills: Identify ways to share your creative talents or skills with others, whether through teaching, volunteering, or offering your services for free. For instance, you could lead an art workshop at a local community center, offer free music lessons to underprivileged children, or donate your graphic design skills to a non-profit organization. Donate an artwork to a community service organization that is raising funds. Alternatively, consider donating part of your art sale proceeds to such an organization. Every little bit (or a large amount) does make a difference.

3. Appreciate and support fellow creatives: Take the time to appreciate and support the creative endeavors of others. Attend art shows, concerts, or exhibitions, and actively engage with the artists by providing thoughtful feedback, purchasing their work, or sharing their creations with your network.

4. Collaborate on community projects: Seek opportunities to collaborate on creative projects that benefit your local community.

This could involve participating in public art installations, community gardens, or neighborhood beautification initiatives. By working together, you contribute to the collective well-being and foster a sense of community and shared purpose.

5. Mentor and inspire others: Share your creative journey and insights with others, particularly younger generations, by serving as a mentor or participating in educational outreach programs. Your guidance and inspiration can ignite the creative spark in others and encourage them to pursue their passions.

6. Cultivate empathy and understanding: Make an effort to understand and appreciate the perspectives, experiences, and struggles of others. Engage in open and respectful dialogues and use your creative expression to foster empathy, understanding, and social change.

These practices help you on your own creative awakening journey and enrich the lives of others. You will gain a deeper sense of purpose, connection, and personal fulfillment. True creative awakening is not a solitary pursuit; it is a journey that intertwines with the world around you. Through acts of generosity and compassion, we can create a ripple effect of positivity and inspiration that extends far beyond our individual selves.

Art as a Means of Self-Expression

Art has long been recognized as a powerful tool for self-expression, allowing artists to communicate their inner thoughts, emotions, and experiences in a profound and transformative way. In the quest for inner peace, self-expression plays a crucial role, enabling creatives to connect with their authentic selves and cultivate a sense of peace.

What exactly is self-expression, though? It sounds kind of "new age" and too alternative to apply to most people. The irony is that it is us regular folks who need this remedy the most. I do not want the benefits of creativity locked away. In case of emergency, "break glass" and extract the creative remedy, apply it, and see your doctor if the problem persists. Jokes aside, this is not how we must look at creative self-expression. Self-expression provides a healthy outlet for emotions and thoughts that may otherwise remain internalized or suppressed. Through artistic expression, individuals can release and process their feelings, offering a cathartic and transformative experience. This does not have to be an earth-shattering experience. For the majority of people, I suspect it will be a moment of peace, relaxation, and contemplation. With time, you may start making connections. You begin to understand yourself better. You start getting insight into what ails you. By giving voice to your innermost feelings, you can experience a sense of emotional release and find inner peace. Self-expression encourages one to fully accept oneself, including strengths, vulnerabilities, and unique qualities. Through self-expression, you can develop greater self-awareness, self-acceptance, and self-worth. Discovering and sharing your authentic voice with the world fosters a deep sense of inner peace and contentment. What is the inner voice? I see this as a sate of mind and living where you are comfortable expressing your views through art. You create and release your art to the world. You are not shy any longer. This state can take a long time to reach, but it could be quick, too. It depends on you and where you are in your journey of self-discovery. Self-expression requires being present in the moment and fully engaged in the creative process. This state of mindful presence brings you into the here and now, temporarily allowing you to let go of worries, anxieties, or stressors. Immersed in self-expression, you experience a calm and focused state of mind, fostering inner peace and a break from the pressures of daily life. It sure beats watching the television! Self-expression is not just a personal journey, but a way to connect with others. By sharing your personal experiences, perspectives, and creative expressions, you can create meaningful connections with others. This sense of connection contributes to a deeper sense of inner peace and fulfillment. When you share something of yourself, you are giving something personal to others. Everyone may not react the same way, but that's not your concern. Your duty is to create and share. Lastly, self-expression allows for the integration of different aspects of one's self—thoughts, emotions, beliefs, values, and experiences. It creates a space where all these dimensions can coexist and be acknowledged. This integration process contributes to a sense of wholeness and completeness, fostering inner peace and a greater understanding of oneself.

Listen More

Paying attention to others and truly listening is an invaluable skill that can enrich our relationships, foster personal growth, and deepen our creative practice. In a world where we are often tempted to showcase our work and accomplishments, active listening can open us up to new perspectives, inspire fresh ideas, and cultivate greater empathy and understanding.

Here are some strategies to help us become better listeners and create space for others to communicate and share their stories:

1. Cultivate presence: When engaging with others, consciously try to be fully present in the moment. Set aside distractions, maintain eye contact, and give the speaker your undivided attention. This simple act of presence communicates respect and creates an environment where the other person feels heard and valued. This is especially true today with the smartphone addiction that plagues us. Are you tired of seeing people staring at their phones while holding a conversation with the person sitting across the table with them? I could go on a tangent here and spend the chapter offloading my frustrations on this topic. But we all get the issue. Now, we need to fix it, and we can start a new awareness of why smartphone addiction is ruining human connection.

2. Practice active listening: Active listening involves more than just hearing words; it's about genuinely comprehending the speaker's message, emotions, and underlying context. Engage in active listening by nodding, asking clarifying questions, and reflecting back on what you've heard to ensure understanding.

3. Suspend judgment: Our preconceived notions or personal biases can often interfere with our ability to listen objectively. Consciously suspend your judgments and assumptions, and approach each conversation with an open mind and a willingness to learn from the other person's perspective.

4. Embrace silence: Many of us feel the need to fill silences with our

thoughts or responses. However, allowing for comfortable pauses can give the speaker time to gather their thoughts and express themselves more fully. Don't be afraid of silence; it can be a powerful tool for active listening.

5. Express genuine curiosity: Ask thoughtful, open-ended questions, encouraging the other person to share more about their experiences, insights, or creative process. Approach these conversations with genuine curiosity and a desire to learn and understand.

6. Validate and affirm: While active listening doesn't necessarily mean agreeing with everything said, it's important to validate the speaker's feelings and experiences. Express empathy, acknowledge their perspective, and affirm their courage in sharing their story.

7. Offer reflective feedback: After listening attentively, consider reflecting back your understanding of the conversation, highlighting key points or insights that resonated with you. This demonstrates your active engagement and allows for clarification and further dialogue. This may suggest a formulaic conversation where you sound fake. No, I do not suggest sounding like a robot parroting sound bites back at the speaker. A little empathy and genuine interest in the conversation will take care of this.

By practicing these listening skills, we not only create space for others to communicate effectively but also open ourselves up to new sources of inspiration and creative enrichment. The stories, perspectives, and experiences shared by others can spark fresh ideas, challenge our assumptions, and deepen our understanding of the human experience—all invaluable ingredients for a rich and fulfilling creative practice.

Ultimately, the art of listening is not just about making others feel heard; it's about cultivating a deeper sense of connection, empathy, and mutual growth – qualities that lie at the heart of a truly meaningful creative awakening.

Avoid the Blame Game

Your life is a reflection of your thoughts. Change your thinking, and you change your life. (Brian Tracy)

undefined

Playing the blame game and perpetually finding fault with others is a significant obstacle that hinders our creative awakening and personal growth. When we adopt a mindset of blame and negativity, we not only damage our relationships and disconnect from others and stifle our creative potential. Instead of wallowing in blame, we must cultivate a mindset of accountability, positivity, and solutions-oriented thinking.

Here are some strategies to help us avoid the blame game and embrace a more constructive approach:

1. Practice self-awareness: Become attuned to your tendency to blame others and consciously catch yourself when you start to engage in this behavior. Take a step back and reflect on the underlying reasons for your blame, whether fear, insecurity, or a need for control. It is easier said than done, but it is a practice that is essential to keeping your life drama-free.

2. Assume positive intent: Instead of immediately assuming the worst or attributing malicious intent to others' actions, strive to assume positive intent. Misunderstandings or conflicts arise from miscommunication or differing perspectives rather than intentional harm. We laugh at others who get "triggered" on social media, for instance, spluttering with indignation as they get more and more heated in the comments section until it is us that gets triggered. It's not a pretty thing to observe.

3. Shift the focus to solutions: Rather than dwelling on who is at fault, redirect your energy towards finding constructive solutions. Ask yourself, "What can I do to improve this situation?" or "How can we move forward positively?" This mindset empowers you to take action

and seek resolutions.

4. Practice active listening: As discussed earlier, it is crucial to actively listen to others without judgment or preconceived notions. When you truly understand someone's perspective, it becomes easier to let go of blame and work towards mutual understanding.

5. Accept accountability: Take ownership of your role in any situation, even if it's a small part. Acknowledge your actions, decisions, or communication breakdowns that may have contributed to the problem. This fosters a sense of personal responsibility and sets an example for others.

6. Cultivate gratitude: Instead of focusing on what went wrong, shift your mindset to gratitude. Appreciate the lessons you can learn from challenging situations, and be grateful for the opportunities for growth and personal development.

7. Surround yourself with positive influences: Seek individuals with a solutions-oriented, positive mindset. Observe how they handle conflicts or setbacks and learn from their example. Positive influences can inspire and reinforce constructive behavior. I have had to rely on books to help me with this aspect. Only by learning from positive people like Dale Carnegie and Brian Tracy and authors like that could I understand what a solutions-driven approach to life looked like. How much better life is when you step back and look for something positive. When you engage your mind on this path, you also help your creative mind take control. The solutions show up, and your life is much better.

8. Complaining all the time can be addictive. You get a few people together; before you know it, someone is starting the same old complaints. It can be difficult at times to avoid doing this. Launching into the latest trigger points is easy, but try to avoid this in a social situation. You could become the "moaning Minnie," people will start feeling down when you bring up all the world's woes. Instead, practice being more positive. Read positive books. Seek and do positive things. Be a creator, and you will have something to inspire others with. It can be life-changing. Everyone loves a little uplifting, positive conversation.

By adopting these strategies, we can break free from the cycle of blame and negativity that often holds us back from our creative potential. When we approach challenges with a mindset of accountability, positivity, and a genuine desire to find solutions, we strengthen our relationships and cultivate an environment that fosters creativity, personal growth, and overall well-being.

Remember, the path to creative awakening is not about assigning blame but embracing our power to shape our experiences and contribute positively to the world. Letting go of the blame game opens ourselves up to new possibilities, deeper connections, and a more fulfilling creative journey.

Art as a Form of Meditation

I have covered aspects of mindfulness while creating and its meditative qualities. This needs a little deeper digging though. Especially for those who struggle with traditional ideas of meditation, like me. Sitting in the lotus position for an hour is not for me, but sitting and painting in my notebook for an hour is bliss. Art has long been recognized for its power to evoke emotions, inspire creativity, and captivate the imagination. However, beyond its aesthetic appeal, art possesses profound meditative qualities that can bring you a sense of calm, focus, and mindfulness. In this chapter, I will explore how art can serve as a form of meditation, quieting your mind and nurturing inner peace.

Art's meditative qualities encompass various aspects, each contributing to a transformative and introspective experience. One of these qualities is the state of presence and mindfulness that art requires. When you engage in the artistic process, you become fully absorbed in the act of creation, bringing your attention to the present moment. Worries and distractions fade, and a sense of focused awareness takes over. In this state, art becomes a gateway to mindfulness, allowing you to immerse yourself in the present moment and find solace in the act of creation.

Another meditative quality of art is the state of flow that it can induce. Flow is a mental state characterized by complete absorption and deep concentration in an activity. When you are in a state of flow, time seems to lose significance, and you become fully engaged and energized by the creative process. This flow-like experience creates a sense of timelessness and a feeling of being fully in the present. Artistic pursuits have the power to transport you into a state of flow, where your actions and awareness merge harmoniously, fostering a deep sense of calm and centeredness.

I will never forget when I was learning more about painting quickly with lots of thick oil paint. I wanted to break out of old habits and explore loose impasto and almost abstract styles of painting. I got started and painted intuitively. I let myself paint freely, glancing at the reference, picking up paint with the brush, and putting it down in a non-stop process from start to finish. After what seemed like a short time, the painting was completed, and I was amazed at the result. Also, I was breathing heavily like I had been on a run. I found this odd because I am not particularly unfit; I had not been running either, but I felt like I had exhausted myself with this painting. I understood that the concentration and engagement in that thirty to forty minutes was a type of flow state. I had focused my mind intently on the subject. I had been moving back and forth, painting while standing up, without letting up, and this had turned into a fair amount of exercise. I felt relaxed and had a sense of achievement that made my day.

Engaging in artistic activities can profoundly impact relaxation and stress reduction. The repetitive motions involved in drawing, painting, or crafting can induce a calming effect similar to meditation. The rhythmic movements, focused attention, and creative expression provide an outlet for emotional release, promote relaxation, and help reduce stress. Art becomes a sanctuary, a space where you can find solace and respite from the demands of daily life.

Art also offers a means of emotional release and catharsis. You can channel your emotions, thoughts, and experiences into your creations through artistic expression. Externalizing and visually representing inner emotions can provide a cathartic release, allowing for emotional healing, self-reflection, and a greater sense of inner peace. Art becomes a transformative tool, enabling you to navigate your emotions and find solace in your creative expressions.

You may tell me, "Malcolm, I had such a frustrating painting session. Nothing would go right, and my painting was a mess".

Trust me, I have those moments, too. Fortunately, these moments are simply part of the process of learning to paint. They are also part of our individual journey. We learn about ourselves—our mental blocks, our emotional frailty. We learn to let go of our expectations and accept that sometimes we make a mess. We need to move on, laugh it off, and create more. Our ego is no longer dominating our minds.

Art and creativity provide a space for self-exploration and introspection. Creating art can lead you to gain insights into your thoughts, feelings, and experiences. It serves as a tool for self-discovery, allowing you to explore your identity, values, and beliefs and fostering a deeper understanding of yourself. Art becomes a mirror, reflecting your inner landscape and offering a pathway to self-awareness and personal growth.

Art offers a non-judgmental space for self-expression, like that situation where your painting looks like a mess. Unlike many other areas of life, art allows you to express yourself freely without fearing being judged or evaluated. This freedom from judgment promotes self-acceptance, encourages authenticity, and fosters a sense of inner peace. Art becomes a sanctuary, a haven where you can fully express yourself without fear or inhibition. It is only your ego you need to worry about. That protective ego creating boogeymen. It is not real. You can see that this painting is not the end but merely a step on the path to self-discovery. Take the next step.

Important: You must protect this safe space like a momma bear protects her cubs. There is no compromise here. Even your significant other can blandly say things that hurt you. You must politely remind them that you do not entertain comments on your art unless requested. Going too far? Not at all. A work in progress can be ruined when an arbitrary remark is made about your work. Nobody needs to "get" what you are exploring at that moment in time—only you. If remarks sway you or influence your flow, you could lose an important direction or exploration.

Engaging the senses is another essential aspect of art as a form of meditation. Art can engage your senses and connect you to the present moment. Whether it's the texture of paint on a canvas, the sound of music, or the smell of clay, artistic activities can heighten sensory awareness and provide a grounding experience. Engaging the senses enhances the meditative quality of the creative process, allowing you to fully immerse yourself in the sensory experience of art. Is that not a wonderful thing? I love the smells of an art studio. The smell of linseed oil. The pastels have their smell. Even ink has a distinctive smell. You must remove toxic fumes from your studio. Turpentine, for example, is no longer necessary. There are non-toxic alternatives. Your studio should be a safe space in every respect.

Lastly, art harmoniously integrates the mind and body. Physically creating art, such as painting, sculpting, or playing a musical instrument, involves a synergy between mental focus, fine motor skills, and creative intuition. This integration of mind and body promotes a sense of balance and unity, enhancing the meditative aspect of the artistic experience. Art becomes a holistic practice, a physical and mental union, fostering a deep connection with yourself and the present moment.

Nurturing Your Creative Spirit: Making Time for Art

In our fast-paced world, finding time for creativity can often feel like an impossible task. The demands of work, family, and other responsibilities can easily consume our days, leaving little room for artistic pursuits. However, nurturing your creative spirit is essential for well-being and personal growth. In this chapter, we will explore practical strategies and mindset shifts that can help you overcome time constraints and prioritize art in your life. The first step in making time for art is recognizing its value in your life. Art is not just a luxury or a frivolous activity; it is a source of personal fulfillment, stress relief, and self-expression. By acknowledging the importance of creativity, you can shift your mindset and make it a non-negotiable part of your routine. Assessing your schedule and commitments is crucial to creating space for art. Take a close look at your daily tasks and activities, identifying any that may be consuming unnecessary time or draining your energy. Consider what you can delegate, eliminate, or reduce to free up more time for creativity. By prioritizing activities that align with your values and well-being, you can create room for art in your life. Treat creative time as you would any other necessary appointment or commitment. Set aside specific blocks of time on your calendar dedicated to artistic pursuits. Whether it's a few minutes each day, a couple of hours during the weekend, or any consistent time that works for you, protect this time and make it a regular practice. Creativity doesn't always require large chunks of time. Embrace micro-moments of creativity throughout your day by keeping a sketchbook or journal. Use short breaks or idle moments to jot down ideas, sketch, or engage in small creative activities. These little bursts of creativity can add up over time and keep your creative energy flowing. An A5 gouache painting can take about thirty minutes. If you keep your painting book, brushes, and a stay-wet palette ready to be used immediately, you can produce a painting daily. This is significant and will do amazing things for your art. Having a dedicated space for your artistic endeavors can enhance your creative experience and make it more convenient to engage in artistic activities. Choose an appropriate location with natural light, ventilation, privacy, and minimal noise. Organize your art supplies and personalize the space with artwork, inspirational quotes, or objects that inspire you. Creating a conducive environment allows you to dive into creative activities and minimize setup time easily. If this is not practical at all at the moment, consider the gouache painting example above. All you need is a desk and chair. Identify periods of the day when you tend to be most productive and creative. Schedule your creative time during these peak productivity periods to maximize your focus and inspiration. You can make the most of your productive time by aligning your artistic pursuits with your natural rhythms. Look for opportunities to integrate creativity into your daily routine. Listen to an audiobook or podcast on creativity while commuting, engage in mindful doodling while on phone calls, or incorporate creative activities into family time or social gatherings. By combining creativity with other activities, you can make art a seamless part of your life. Minimize distractions that interrupt your time and prevent you from engaging in creative pursuits. Create boundaries by turning off notifications on your devices, setting specific times for email and social media, and creating a conducive environment that supports your focus and creativity. By reducing distractions, you can create a space for deep artistic exploration. Distractions are the killers of creativity. If finding significant chunks of time for art feels challenging, start with small and manageable increments. Even 10 minutes a day dedicated to creativity can make a difference. The key is consistency. Establish a routine and commit to showing up regularly for your creative practice. Starting small and being consistent can build momentum and make art a natural part of your life. Nurturing your creative spirit requires intention, prioritization, and a willingness to carve out space for something that brings you joy and fulfillment. By implementing these strategies and mindset shifts, you can overcome time constraints and create a regular practice of creativity. Remember, making time for art is a personal commitment that requires dedication and perseverance. With a proactive approach and a mindset focused on nurturing your creative spirit, you can prioritize art and experience the transformative power of creativity.

The question is always: "How badly do you want to do this?"

The Healing Power of Art Therapy

Art has long been recognized as a powerful medium for self-expression and emotional release. Through art, individuals can communicate thoughts, emotions, and experiences that may be challenging to put into words. Creating art can provide a safe space for self-reflection and exploration, facilitating emotional healing and promoting overall well-being. There are different approaches to art therapy. One option is seeking help from a certified professional who incorporates art therapy into a professional practice. The other route is for less severe mental issues that will benefit from art in the typical form we understand. Painting at home, in workshops, and so on. There is an overlap. Art can become an essential aspect of one's life for years after formal therapy has ended. Engaging in art offers numerous therapeutic benefits that can positively impact mental, emotional, and even physical well-being. One key therapeutic benefit of art is its ability to serve as an outlet for self-expression. Creating art allows individuals to communicate their innermost thoughts and feelings, providing a powerful means of emotional release. By externalizing their emotions through art, individuals can gain insights, perspective, and resolution, contributing to emotional healing and well-being. Art also serves as a form of relaxation and stress relief. Creating art promotes a state of flow—complete immersion and absorption in the artistic activity. This immersion in the creative process can calm the mind, reduce anxiety, and promote a sense of calm and well-being. Engaging in art can serve as a healthy distraction from everyday worries and stressors, redirecting attention to the creative process and promoting relaxation and rejuvenation. Furthermore, art therapy fosters increased self-awareness and self-understanding. Through creating art, individuals often discover new aspects of themselves, uncover hidden strengths, or gain clarity about their values and beliefs.

The act of creating art can also boost self-esteem and confidence. As individuals engage in artistic activities and witness their creative abilities, they experience a sense of accomplishment and pride in their work. This positive reinforcement contributes to an increased sense of self-worth and belief in one's abilities.

Artistic activities require focus, concentration, and being fully present in the moment. Engaging in art promotes mindfulness, as individuals immerse themselves in the process, observe details, and engage their senses. This mindful engagement enhances present-moment awareness, fostering a sense of grounding and connection. Art therapy, a specialized form that utilizes art-making and creative processes, can be particularly effective in helping individuals process emotions and traumas. It provides a nonverbal outlet for expressing emotions and experiences that may be difficult to put into words. Through art-making, individuals can externalize and symbolically represent their feelings, memories, and traumas. Using symbolism and metaphor in art therapy allows for the exploration and communication of complex emotions or traumatic events in a safe and manageable way. Art therapy can also provide a cathartic experience, allowing individuals to release pent-up emotions and find relief. Externalizing and objectifying internal experiences through art-making creates a sense of distance and objectivity, enabling individuals to explore and process traumatic experiences. Art therapy empowers individuals by giving them a sense of control over their creative process, helping to rebuild a sense of agency and empowerment. Art therapy also facilitates the process of integrating fragmented or disorganized experiences related to trauma. Through art-making, individuals can gain a sense of coherence, understanding, and meaning from their traumatic experiences. Art therapy helps regulate and stabilize emotions and the nervous system, promoting a sense of calm and safety. The therapeutic relationship between the art therapist and the individual is crucial to art therapy. The art therapist creates a safe and supportive environment for individuals to explore their emotions and traumas. The art therapist guides and facilitates the art-making process through empathy, validation, and insight, helping individuals navigate their healing journey. Art therapy is effective in various contexts. It has been utilized to help individuals heal from traumatic experiences, support mental health and well-being, work with individuals on the autism spectrum, assist individuals with dementia and aging, and cope with grief and loss. Individuals can take practical steps to explore art therapy and its healing power. Researching and educating oneself about art therapy and its potential benefits is a crucial first step. Seeking professional guidance from a certified art therapist or mental health professional specializing in art therapy is essential. Attending art therapy workshops or groups can provide firsthand experience and an opportunity to connect with others. If formal art therapy sessions are not accessible, incorporating art into daily life as a self-guided therapeutic activity can still be beneficial. Creating a supportive environment that encourages artistic expression and exploration is also important. Art therapy harnesses the power of creativity, artistic expression, and the therapeutic relationship to help individuals process emotions and traumas. By engaging in art-making, individuals can access deeper levels of self-awareness, promote emotional healing, and develop resilience in the face of trauma. Whether through formal art therapy sessions or self-guided artistic activities, art has the potential to be a transformative tool for self-care, personal growth, and overall well-being.

Embracing Imperfection: The Beauty of Flaws

Many artists are trapped in a relentless quest for perfection in their pursuit of artistic excellence. They strive for flawless execution, impeccable technique, and impeccable outcomes. However, this ruthless pursuit of perfection can stifle creativity, hinder self-expression, and rob artists of the joy of the creative process. This chapter will explore the importance of embracing imperfections and mistakes as part of the artistic process and how doing so can lead to greater creativity, self-acceptance, personal growth, and creative fulfillment. Embracing imperfections and mistakes is crucial for several reasons. Firstly, it allows for growth and learning. Artistic development involves experimentation, taking risks, and pushing boundaries. Mistakes provide valuable opportunities to learn from the process, discover new techniques, and refine skills. Embracing imperfections fosters a growth mindset, encouraging artists to see challenges as stepping stones toward improvement. Secondly, embracing imperfections helps artists embrace their unique style and voice. Perfectionism can stifle creativity and hinder the expression of genuine emotions and ideas. Many perfectionists stop with art entirely when they get caught up in all the emotional angst. Who needs that? Nobody, so they give up art instead of becoming self-aware and healing the perfectionist tendency. Accepting imperfections allows for a more authentic and personal artistic expression, enabling artists to stay true to their vision and embrace their individuality. Furthermore, embracing imperfections cultivates flexibility and adaptability, allowing artists to respond creatively to unforeseen circumstances. It encourages artists to adapt their original plans, incorporate mistakes into their artwork, and find innovative solutions to artistic challenges. Embracing imperfections also frees artists from the pressure of achieving flawless results, allowing them to explore and experiment without fear of judgment or failure. Embracing imperfections also contributes to emotional resilience. Art-making can evoke strong emotions, and accepting imperfections can also contribute to emotional resilience. Artistic pursuits are not immune to setbacks and frustrations, but accepting imperfections helps artists develop emotional resilience and cope with setbacks in a healthier way. It allows for self-compassion, reduces self-criticism, and promotes a more positive and constructive artistic experience. Embracing imperfections shifts the focus from the end result to the creative process itself. By valuing the journey and the learning experience, artists can engage more fully in the present moment, fostering mindfulness and enjoyment. This process-oriented focus promotes a deeper connection with the artistic process and allows for greater creative exploration and discovery. Finally, embracing imperfections can lead to unexpected breakthroughs and innovative ideas. Often, mistakes can spark new directions, alternative techniques, or unique artistic solutions. By accepting imperfections, artists open themselves up to serendipitous moments and the potential for groundbreaking artistic discoveries. You can employ several strategies to let go of the need for perfection and embrace the beauty of imperfection. Firstly, shift your perspective and challenge the belief that perfection is the ultimate goal. By recognizing that imperfections bring character and uniqueness to your work, you can shift your focus from seeking flawlessness to valuing growth, authenticity, and personal expression. Another important point is to embrace the learning process and see each piece of work as an opportunity to learn, experiment, and develop skills. Embracing the journey of growth and improvement and understanding that mistakes and imperfections are essential for progress can help you let go of the need for perfection. Setting realistic expectations is another important strategy. Understanding that perfection is unattainable and setting challenging yet attainable goals allows room for exploration and learning. Regardless of achieving flawless outcomes, celebrating progress along the way is crucial for embracing imperfections. Practicing self-compassion is also essential. Treating oneself with kindness and understanding, being mindful of self-talk, and replacing self-critical thoughts with self-encouragement can help individuals embrace imperfections. Recognizing that imperfections are natural and part of the creative process and treating oneself with patience and understanding fosters self-compassion. Another effective strategy is to embrace mistakes as learning opportunities. Viewing mistakes as valuable learning opportunities, embracing the insights and knowledge that can arise from exploring and correcting errors, and seeing mistakes as stepping stones to improvement and growth rather than as failures can help individuals let go of the fear of making mistakes. Furthermore, individuals can experiment and take risks by stepping out of their comfort zones. Allowing oneself to try new techniques, explore different styles, and experiment with unconventional ideas gives permission to make mistakes and see them as opportunities for discovery and innovation. Focusing on progress rather than perfection is essential for embracing imperfections. Celebrating progress and the small victories along the way, acknowledging improvements made, skills developed, and lessons learned, regardless of any imperfections that may still exist, is crucial for letting go of the need for perfection. Surrounding oneself with imperfection is another effective strategy. Engaging with artwork, literature, or music that embraces imperfection and celebrates uniqueness, seeking inspiration from artists who value authenticity and are known for their distinct style, and engaging with creative communities or support groups that promote self-acceptance and appreciation of imperfections can help individuals embrace imperfection. Embracing imperfections can lead to personal growth and artistic fulfillment in various ways. First, it fosters self-acceptance by allowing you to acknowledge and embrace your unique qualities, quirks, and artistic style. Second, it frees you from the constant pursuit of perfection, cultivating a sense of self-worth and self-compassion. I can say that this acceptance keeps me grounded. My garage has piles of old painting panels. These are paintings that are not good enough to make it onto my website. I can reuse the old panels or, if that is not possible, throw them out. I can see how far I have come and how far I still intend to go. I can never get too big for my own boots, because these failed paintings remind me that I am still learning and will continue to learn for the rest of my life. Secondly, embracing imperfections encourages artists to step outside their comfort zones and explore new artistic possibilities. When the fear of making mistakes or falling short of perfection is diminished, artists are more willing to take risks, experiment with different techniques, and push the boundaries of their creativity. This openness to exploration fosters artistic growth and fulfillment. Furthermore, embracing imperfections develops resilience and adaptability. Artists encounter challenges, setbacks, and artistic blocks throughout their creative journey. By embracing imperfections, artists learn to persevere, adapt, and find creative solutions. They become more resilient in the face of obstacles, bounce back from setbacks, and grow through the process. Embracing imperfections allows you to express your true self authentically. It encourages you to create without the burden of meeting external expectations or conforming to ideals of perfection. Artists who embrace imperfections feel more comfortable expressing their emotions, unique perspectives, and personal experiences through their art. This authenticity in expression leads to a more profound sense of fulfillment and connection with their creative work. Additionally, embracing imperfections nurtures a growth mindset—a belief in one's ability to learn, improve, and grow. Artists who accept imperfections as part of the creative process view mistakes as opportunities for learning and growth. This commitment to learning fosters personal growth and fulfillment as artists progress on their artistic journey. Finally, embracing imperfections invites a sense of joy and creative freedom. When artists let go of the need for perfection, they can enjoy the process of creating without self-imposed pressure or criticism. They experience the joy of exploration, playfulness, and spontaneity in their art. Embracing imperfections allows artists to fully immerse themselves in the creative process, leading to a sense of fulfillment and satisfaction. As I mentioned before, do not take this state of being for granted. Protect it from negativity and the naysayers. It is a fragile state of creative harmony that is precious to you.

Art and Community: Finding Connection and Support

Artistic journeys are often solitary endeavors, with artists spending countless hours in their studios, immersed in their creative process. However, the importance of community in the artistic journey should not be underestimated. Being part of a creative community provides you with a supportive and encouraging network that plays a significant role in your artistic growth and fulfillment. One of the key benefits of being part of a community is the support and encouragement it offers. Fellow artists, mentors, and art enthusiasts within the community can provide guidance, constructive feedback, and emotional support throughout the artistic journey. They understand the challenges, triumphs, and frustrations that artists experience and can offer a sense of camaraderie and understanding. Collaboration is another powerful aspect of community involvement. By collaborating with peers on projects, exhibitions, or creative endeavors, artists bring diverse perspectives and skills together. These collaborative experiences can spark new ideas, challenge artistic boundaries, and push individuals to explore new techniques or concepts. Through interaction, artists gain fresh insights, inspiration, and a broader artistic perspective. Learning and skill development are also facilitated within the artistic community. Workshops, classes, or mentorship programs offer valuable resources for acquiring new techniques, refining artistic skills, and expanding artistic knowledge. Sharing knowledge and experiences allows for mutual growth and development as artists learn from one another. Being part of a creative community also opens doors to networking and professional opportunities. Through community events, exhibitions, or online platforms, artists can connect with galleries, art organizations, and potential clients or buyers. Networking within the community can lead to collaborations, exhibition opportunities, commissions, and career advancement. Feedback and critique are essential for artistic growth, and a community of artists provides a space for constructive feedback and critique. Peers and mentors can offer insights, suggestions, and perspectives on artistic work. This feedback helps artists refine their skills, identify areas for improvement, and gain a fresh perspective on their creative process.

Constructive critique from the community fosters growth and elevates the quality of artistic output. Beyond the practical benefits, being part of an artistic community creates a sense of belonging. Artists can connect with like-minded individuals with similar passions, experiences, and aspirations. The community's sense of belonging and shared identity enhances confidence, self-esteem, and motivation. It reduces feelings of isolation and provides a support system during challenging times. Exposure and recognition are also heightened within the artistic community. Artists can showcase their work in community exhibitions, events, or online platforms, reaching a broader audience. The community can amplify an artist's visibility and recognition, opening doors to new opportunities, collaborations, and potential buyers or collectors. Emotional well-being is another crucial aspect of community engagement in the artistic journey. Connection with others who understand the creative process and share similar passions provides emotional support, reduces feelings of isolation, and enhances overall mental and emotional health. The sense of community fosters a sense of purpose, fulfillment, and connection, contributing to artists' overall well-being. Finding like-minded individuals and creating a support network within the artistic community can be achieved through various strategies. Attending local art events, joining art organizations and groups, taking art classes or workshops, utilizing online platforms, attending art retreats or residencies, collaborating on projects, engaging in online challenges or prompts, and organizing meetups or studio visits are all effective ways to connect with fellow artists and build a supportive community. Collaborative artistic endeavors offer numerous benefits for artists. Collaboration brings together individuals with different backgrounds, perspectives, and artistic styles, enriching the creative process. It allows for mutual learning, skill development, and expanded creativity. Collaborative projects provide emotional support, shared resources, enhanced problem-solving skills, mutual inspiration, and amplified impact. I have experienced the transformative power of community and collaboration in my artistic journey. Being part of a community has provided me with a network of like-minded individuals who understand the joys and struggles of the creative process. The support, encouragement, and feedback I have received from fellow artists have been invaluable in my growth as an artist. Collaborative projects have also been a source of inspiration and growth for me. Working with other artists has pushed me out of my comfort zone, encouraging me to explore new techniques and ideas. The diverse perspectives and skills brought by my collaborators have enriched my work and expanded my creative horizons. Being part of a community has contributed to my artistic growth and brought me a sense of fulfillment. The connections and relationships formed within the creative community have enhanced my overall well-being and provided me with a support system that sustains me during challenging times. Being part of a community is essential for artistic growth and fulfillment. The support, collaboration, inspiration, learning opportunities, networking, feedback, recognition, sense of belonging, and emotional well-being that come from community involvement enhance the artistic experience. The connections and relationships formed within the creative community foster growth, provide a sense of purpose and contribute to the artist's overall fulfillment and success.

Art as a Catalyst for Personal Growth and Transformation

Art has the power to inspire personal growth and self-discovery in profound ways. Through various forms, art becomes a vehicle for your self-expression, exploration of your identity, emotional release and healing, challenging your comfort zones, building your self-confidence and empowerment, shifting your perspectives and cultivating empathy, and fostering your reflection and meaning-making. Engaging in artistic pursuits allows you to embark on a transformative journey of self-exploration, enabling you to grow, evolve, and discover new aspects of yourself.

I've come to realize that using art as a tool for introspection and self-reflection allows me to delve into my inner self and gain a deeper understanding of my thoughts, emotions, and experiences. Visual journaling provides me with a dedicated space for self-reflection through art, allowing me to express my thoughts, emotions, and experiences visually.

Self-portraiture, for example, captures not only your physical likeness but also delves into your psyche, capturing your mood, inner thoughts, or self-perception. Abstract artists find that abstract and non-representational art forms provide them with the freedom to express emotions, thoughts, or experiences without relying on realistic depictions. Creating art as a means of emotional release has been a cathartic outlet for my emotions and a way to process my inner experiences, and I can do the same for you, too. Engaging in artistic rituals or incorporating meditative practices into my creative process has deepened my self-reflection and introspection. Through engaging in a dialogue with my own artwork, I gain insights, question assumptions, and explore the deeper meanings behind my creative expressions. There are countless stories of individuals who have experienced transformative journeys through art. Artists who have used art as a means of self-expression and exploration have discovered hidden talents challenged societal norms and embraced their authentic selves. Through art, individuals have found healing and emotional release, gaining insights into their emotional landscapes and fostering personal growth. By stepping outside their comfort zones and embracing new challenges, artists have developed resilience, adaptability, and a willingness to embrace growth and change. Engaging with art from diverse cultures, styles, and perspectives has broadened individuals' worldviews and fostered empathy, understanding, and appreciation for diverse experiences and viewpoints. Through reflection and meaning-making, individuals have found personal significance in their experiences and deepened their understanding of themselves and the world around them. To use art for personal growth and self-discovery, you can take practical steps to incorporate these aspects into your artistic practice. Setting aside dedicated time for self-reflection, experimenting with different mediums and techniques, choosing personal projects or themes, engaging in mindful art-making practices, seeking feedback and constructive critique, establishing artistic rituals and creative habits, and joining art communities or engaging in collaborative projects are all ways to harness the transformative potential of art. By being intentional, engaging in self-reflection, embracing authenticity, exploring and experimenting, cultivating mindfulness and presence, reflecting on artwork, creating a supportive environment, being open to change, and practicing persistence and patience, you can use art as a catalyst for personal growth and transformation. Art can awaken our inner selves, unlocking hidden truths and fostering personal growth. Through self-expression, exploration, emotional release, and reflection, art becomes a catalyst for personal transformation. By engaging in artistic pursuits and embracing the transformative potential of art, individuals embark on a journey of self-discovery, self-expression, and self-growth. Art becomes a powerful tool for introspection, allowing you to delve into your inner landscapes, gain insights, and deepen your understanding of yourself and the world around you.

The Role of Art in Cultivating Mindfulness in Everyday Life

In the hustle and bustle of our daily lives, finding moments of calm and presence can be challenging. However, incorporating art as a reminder to stay present and mindful can be a powerful tool in cultivating mindfulness throughout our daily activities. We can connect deeply with ourselves and the world by infusing art into our mindfulness practice. When I say "the world," I am not referring to the endless loop of social media, news broadcasts, gossip, and the thousands of daily distractions. I mean connecting with nature, our universal connections with our environment. That awareness that we are part of the living world. This chapter will explore various techniques, examples, and practical ways to use art in cultivating mindfulness in our everyday lives. Using art as a reminder to stay present and mindful during the day can effectively cultivate mindfulness throughout your daily activities. Here are some techniques and methods to incorporate art into your mindfulness practice: **Create Art Affirmations**: One technique is writing short affirmations or meaningful quotes related to mindfulness or presence on small cards or sticky notes. Decorate these cards with artistic elements such as drawings, colors, or patterns. Place them in visible locations, such as your workspace, bathroom mirror, or refrigerator, as gentle reminders to stay present and mindful. **Mindful Doodling**: Another technique is to keep a sketchbook or notepad with you during the day. Whenever you have a moment or feel the need to refocus, engage in mindful doodling. Allow your pen or pencil to move freely on the page without specific intention. Pay attention to the sensations, lines, and shapes you create. This simple act of doodling can help anchor you in the present moment. If you grew up in the pre-digital era you may have spent a lot of time doing this in your school books. That was me – filling every margin with doodles. Did me no harm. **Daily Sketching or Art Journaling**: Set aside a specific time each day to engage in mindful sketching or art journaling. This dedicated practice encourages you to attentively observe your surroundings and inner experiences. Focus on capturing the present moment's details, emotions, or sensations through your artistic expression. It could be a quick sketch of an object, a scene, or a visual representation of your thoughts and feelings.

I love doing this so much that I created a course on journaling with various media. My desk always has a few small watercolor sketchbooks for impromptu gouache or watercolor painting. Doing these small studies while listening to music has to be one of the greatest escapes possible. **Mandalas or Zentangles**: Create mandalas or engage in the practice of Zentangle, a method of drawing structured patterns. These art forms offer a meditative experience as you focus on repetitive patterns, shapes, and lines. Use them as a mindful activity to center yourself and promote a sense of calm and presence. **Mindful Coloring**: Engage in mindful coloring activities with adult coloring books or by creating your own mandalas or intricate patterns. Approach coloring as a meditative practice, paying attention to your hand's sensations, colors, and movements as you fill the spaces with color. Allow the act of coloring to be soothing and a reminder to stay present. **Artistic Mindfulness Reminders**: Incorporate visual reminders of mindfulness or presence into your everyday objects or surroundings. For example, you can paint a small symbol or word related to mindfulness on your coffee mug, place a piece of artwork or an inspirational quote on your desk, or create a small art piece to hang by your front door. These reminders serve as prompts to pause, take a breath, and reconnect with the present moment. **Engage in Art-Based Meditation**: Combine art and meditation practices by using art-based meditation techniques, such as guided visualization exercises or mandala meditation. These practices encourage a focused and calm state of mind, allowing you to tap into your creativity while staying present and mindful.

By infusing art into our daily routines, we can experience the following benefits: **Stress Reduction**: Mindful engagement in artistic activities helps reduce stress and promote relaxation. When we focus on creating art and stay present in the process, our minds shift away from stressors and worries. This redirection of attention can lead to a calmer state of mind, reducing stress levels and promoting overall well-being. **Increased Self-Awareness**: Engaging in art with mindfulness enhances self-awareness. We gain a deeper understanding of ourselves by staying present and observing our thoughts, emotions, and sensations while creating art. This increased self-awareness allows us to recognize and respond to our needs, desires, and feelings more effectively, improving well-being. **Enhanced Emotional Well-being**: Artistic expression and mindfulness combined promote emotional well-being. Art provides a means to express and process emotions in a healthy and constructive way. By staying present and aware of our emotions during art-making, we can better understand and manage them, improving emotional balance and resilience. **Improved Focus and Concentration**: Engaging in art mindfully trains our minds to focus and concentrate on the task. This practice of sustained attention can carry over to other areas of life, enhancing productivity and efficiency. Improved focus and concentration contribute to a sense of accomplishment and well-being. **Cultivation of Positive Mindset**: Combining art and mindfulness can shift our mindset towards positivity. Mindfulness encourages non-judgmental acceptance of thoughts and emotions, while art offers a platform for self-expression and creative exploration. This combination promotes a positive outlook, fostering a sense of gratitude, self-compassion, and optimism, which are vital components of overall well-being. Knowing why you are doing something creative and how you want to be is essential. If you do something creative but spend your time steaming over some event or are anxious about something to the point of distraction, then you are not self-aware. You are losing any benefit from the creative task. You may not even be aware of what you are doing. Constantly check in with yourself to ensure you know what is bothering you and try to detach from those emotions. Let them pass as you turn your attention to the creative task. **Increased Resilience**: Engaging in art as a reminder to stay present and mindful nurtures resilience. Mindfulness helps develop the ability to respond to challenges with greater awareness and adaptability. Artistic expression provides a creative outlet for processing and reframing experiences, allowing us to bounce back from difficulties and cultivate resilience in the face of adversity. **Connection with Inner Self and Authenticity**: Integrating art and mindfulness supports a deeper connection with our inner selves and fosters authenticity. By staying present and engaged in the creative process, we can tap into our true thoughts, emotions, and desires, nurturing a sense of authenticity and alignment with our core values. This connection with our inner selves contributes to greater well-being and fulfillment. Imagine how much better your relationships, work-life balance, and emotional health will be when you escape the triggers that keep you distracted, anxious, and defensive. Incorporating art into our mindfulness practice can help us live more balanced and fulfilling lives.

Whether through mindful doodling, daily sketching, or engaging in art-based meditation, the act of creating art with mindfulness allows us to tap into our creativity, express ourselves authentically, and cultivate a deep sense of presence and peace. So why not pick up a pen, a paintbrush, or colored pencils and let the creative awakening begin?

The Creative Awakening: A Call to Action

This chapter will explore the practical steps you can take to embrace your creativity, step away from the digital world, and reconnect with your creative spirit. We will also delve into the transformative potential of art in troubled times and the key elements of a creative awakening. The journey towards embracing creativity and prioritizing artistic pursuits is a path that leads to joy and fulfillment. It requires a combination of mindset shifts, practical strategies, and self-reflection. It begins with cultivating a creative mindset that recognizes the inherent human capacity for creativity and values its importance in our lives. In short, you need to believe in our art and let go of the cynical mindset that the world has on this topic. Have we always been this anxious about everything? I believe we are being pushed into this unbalanced state. Once we find our footing again, we can see the answer. Our art and creativity are part of that answer. To embark on this journey, it is crucial to identify and challenge any blocks or limiting beliefs that have hindered our creative pursuits in the past. Recognizing and overcoming these barriers is essential, whether it be fear of judgment, self-doubt, or the belief that we are not "talented" enough. We must shift our focus from pursuing perfection to embracing the creation process, allowing ourselves to experiment, make mistakes, and learn from them. Setting clear intentions and goals for our creative journey helps solidify our commitment and provides direction. By creating a dedicated space and time for our artistic pursuits, we establish an environment that nurtures our creativity and minimizes distractions. Starting small and building momentum allows us to develop a consistent creative practice while seeking inspiration and learning opportunities from other artists, and the art community reignites our creative spark. Community is important. We are part of a community, and you are part of the community of artists. Isolation is not healthy. Accountability and support from like-minded individuals are not just beneficial, they are essential in our creative journey. Finding an accountability partner or joining a creative group or community provides not only encouragement and motivation, but also a sense of belonging. Letting go of judgment and comparison is essential, as it allows us to embrace our own artistic voice, value our creative process, and celebrate our individual growth and progress. Stepping away from the digital world and reconnecting with our creative spirit is a valuable practice for cultivating creativity and focus. We can create a healthier balance between digital engagement and artistic endeavors by setting clear boundaries, creating a digital-free zone, and scheduling dedicated time for offline creative pursuits. Disconnecting from notifications, establishing a pre-creative routine, and practicing digital detoxes further minimize distractions and allow us to immerse ourselves in the creative process fully. Personal experiences and examples of individuals who have embraced their creativity and found fulfillment serve as powerful reminders of the transformative potential of art. Read the biographies or autobiographies of artists you admire. None had an easy life escaping obscurity or simply making a living. It is hard before it gets easier. Pushing through the hard part is essential. These stories remind us that we are part of a long community of creatives. In troubled times, it is important to remind ourselves of the transformative potential of art. By setting reminders, creating visual cues, establishing a creative break routine, using creative prompts, collaborating with a creative buddy, creating a creative break kit, practicing mindful self-check-ins, and creating rituals, we can prompt ourselves to take creative breaks when we feel troubled. These breaks provide an opportunity for rejuvenation, problem-solving, and self-care. Embracing creativity and prioritizing artistic pursuits require a combination of mindset shifts, practical strategies, and self-reflection. We can cultivate creativity, focus, and well-being by stepping away from the digital world and reconnecting with our creative spirit. The transformative potential of art in troubled times serves as a reminder of the power of creativity to navigate through challenges and find solace and fulfillment. By embracing our creativity, we embark on a journey of self-expression, personal growth, and inner peace.

The Journey Continues: Sustaining Your Creative Awakening

As we embark on our creative journey, we may wonder how to sustain our passion and continue to find fulfillment in our artistic pursuits. The path of creativity is not always smooth, and challenges and obstacles can arise along the way. However, with the right mindset and strategies, we can overcome these hurdles and brighten the flame of our creative awakening. Setting realistic goals is one of the first strategies in sustaining our creative practice. By establishing achievable and manageable goals, we can maintain a sense of progress and accomplishment. Breaking down larger goals into smaller tasks allows us to stay motivated and engaged, even when faced with daunting projects. This sense of progress fuels our momentum and keeps us on track. Creating a routine is another essential aspect of sustaining our creative awakening. By designating specific days or times each week for our creative practice, we treat them as non-negotiable appointments with ourselves. Consistency is key to building momentum and making our creative hobby a consistent part of our lives. Adhering to a routine creates a sense of discipline and dedication to our craft.

I regard setting a routine as so important that I want to explore this topic a little deeper right now by looking at five good tips that will help you.

These are five tried and tested tips for artists to develop a creative routine:

1. Set Specific Goals

Tip: Define clear and achievable goals for your creative practice. Whether completing a sketch each day, working on a painting for a certain number of hours per week, or experimenting with new techniques, having specific goals helps provide direction and motivation.

Implementation: Write down your goals and break them into smaller, manageable tasks. Track your progress regularly to stay motivated and accountable.

2. Designate a Dedicated Workspace

Tip: Create a dedicated space for your art. Having a specific area reserved for your creative work can help you mentally switch into "creative mode" and reduce distractions.

Implementation: Organize your workspace with all the necessary supplies and ensure it's comfortable and inspiring. Keep it tidy to avoid clutter that might disrupt your focus. No space? Consider that I had to make do with a corner of our bedroom for about a year. I had the support of my wife, which is essential, but this meant dealing with occasional paint drops on the floor and even the wall! Yes, I used acrylics, which helps. If I used gouache it would have been even simpler. So do what you must, and your world will accommodate your growing career. Start with what you have.

3. Schedule Regular Creative Time

Tip: As mentioned above, treat your creative practice like any other important appointment. Schedule specific weekly days and times to work on your art and make these sessions non-negotiable.

Implementation: Use a planner or digital calendar to block out these times. Consistency is key, so start with manageable time slots, like 30 minutes a day, and gradually increase as it becomes a habit.

4. Start with a Warm-Up Routine

Tip: Begin each session with a simple, relaxing activity to get into the creative mindset. This could be doodling, stretching, or listening to music.

Implementation: Develop a short, enjoyable routine that you do every time before starting your main project. This helps signal your brain that it's time to focus on creative work. Music is important to me as it improves my energy and focus. Spotify or YouTube Music makes it easy to create your mix-tape session, and it is fun to do. Alternatively, your CD collection could do with some dusting off to get you into the mood. I avoid playing movies, though. I do not want to be distracted by TV of any sort.

5. Eliminate Distractions

Tip: Identify and minimize distractions that can interrupt your creative flow. This includes digital distractions, noise, and even personal interruptions.

Implementation: Turn off notifications on your devices, set boundaries with people around you, and consider using noise-canceling headphones or ambient music to maintain focus.

Establishing a Routine

How long it takes to establish a routine can vary from person to person, but on average, it takes about 21 days to form a new habit, though some studies suggest it can take up to 66 days for a behavior to become automatic. Consistency and dedication are crucial during this period. Here are some additional tips to help:

Be Patient and Flexible: Understand that forming a routine takes time and may have setbacks. Be patient with yourself and flexible enough to adjust the routine if needed.

Celebrate Small Wins: Acknowledge and celebrate your progress along the way. This positive reinforcement can help you stay motivated.

Track Your Progress: Use a journal or a habit-tracking app to record your creative sessions. Visualizing your progress can be very encouraging.

By following these tips and giving yourself time to adjust, you can develop a sustainable and rewarding creative routine that enhances your artistic practice and overall well-being. Never give up!

Embracing variety is crucial in avoiding creative ruts. Exploring different techniques, subjects, or styles keeps our practice fresh and exciting. Experimenting with new materials or approaches can reignite our passion and find ongoing inspiration. Embracing variety allows us to evolve as artists continuously and keeps our creative fire burning.

Seeking inspiration from various sources is another powerful strategy for sustaining our creative awakening. By surrounding ourselves with art, whether through following artists on social media, visiting exhibitions, or reading books about art, we expose ourselves to diverse forms of inspiration. Engaging with different artistic styles and movements keeps our creative spirit alive and provides us with new ideas for our work. I love art books about artists or art movements that interest me. Have fun with your learning. It is not an exam topic, and there are no tests. Art is fascinating when you discover more about these aspects. Joining a creative community or art group is another effective way to sustain our creative practice. By connecting with fellow artists who share our passion, we gain a support system that provides encouragement, accountability, and the opportunity to learn and grow together. Attending workshops and art classes or joining online forums allows us to share ideas, seek feedback, and collaborate. Being part of a community fosters a sense of belonging and provides the motivation to continue our artistic journey. Celebrating small wins is an essential mindset to sustain our creative awakening. Acknowledging and taking pride in our progress, no matter how small, boosts our motivation and fosters a positive mindset. By recognizing the effort we put into our creative practice, we cultivate a sense of fulfillment and satisfaction. Celebrating small wins encourages us to continue our artistic journey with enthusiasm and joy. Embracing the learning process is vital in sustaining our creative practice. Understanding that learning and growth are inherent parts of the creative process allows us to embrace mistakes, challenges, and setbacks as opportunities for improvement. By approaching our practice with a growth mindset, we view every experience as a chance to develop and refine our skills. This mindset keeps us engaged and motivated, even in the face of obstacles. Maintaining a balance between discipline and playfulness is another key to sustaining our creative awakening. While it is important to have a dedicated work ethic and commitment to our craft, allowing ourselves space for exploration, experimentation, and play keeps the process enjoyable. By finding this balance, we keep our creativity alive and maintain our engagement in the long term. Taking breaks when needed is crucial in sustaining our creative practice. Sometimes, stepping away from our creative hobby for a short period can rekindle our enthusiasm. During these breaks, we can rest, recharge, and explore other interests. Returning to our creative practice with fresh eyes and renewed energy reignites our passion and motivation. Regularly reflecting on why we started our creative hobby in the first place is a powerful tool for sustaining our creative awakening. By reconnecting with our initial motivations, we remind ourselves of the value and importance of our creative practice. This reflection keeps us focused and committed over the long term, even during doubt or difficulty. Sustaining our creative awakening requires commitment, patience, and a willingness to navigate the ups and downs. By implementing these strategies and adapting them to our individual needs, we can keep the momentum going and enjoy the benefits and fulfillment of our creative pursuits. Our journey continues, and we grow as artists and individuals with each step.

Celebrating Your Creative Self: Showcasing Your Art

The act of creating art is a deeply personal and introspective journey. It allows us to tap into our innermost thoughts, emotions, and experiences and express them visually. But what happens when we take our creations out into the world? What happens when we share our art with others, celebrate our creative selves, and showcase our artistic creations? In this chapter, we will explore the importance of sharing and celebrating our art, the various ways we can exhibit our work and connect with others, and the joy and fulfillment of sharing our creativity. Sharing your artistic journey and creations is important for several reasons. First, it allows you to connect with others who share similar interests and passions. Second, by sharing your art, you create a sense of community where you can engage in meaningful conversations, receive feedback, and gain support from like-minded individuals. Building connections with fellow artists and art enthusiasts can provide inspiration, encouragement, and opportunities for collaboration. Secondly, sharing your work invites constructive feedback and critique from others. This feedback can provide valuable insights and perspectives that help you refine your skills, expand your creative vision, and identify areas for improvement. Opening yourself up to feedback can accelerate your growth as an artist and continually evolve your artistic practice. Furthermore, sharing your artistic creations allows you to receive validation and recognition for your work. Positive feedback, praise, and acknowledgment from others can boost your confidence, reaffirm your artistic abilities, and validate the importance of your creative endeavors. It can serve as motivation to keep pushing forward and exploring new artistic possibilities. But sharing your art is not just about receiving validation and recognition. It is also about inspiring and influencing others. Your artistic journey and creations can ignite the creativity and passion of those who encounter your work. By sharing your unique perspective, techniques, and creative process, you can spark ideas and encourage others to explore their own artistic endeavors. Sharing your art can make a powerful impact on individuals and society. It allows you to address social issues, express your beliefs, and provoke thought and reflection. Your art can evoke emotions, challenge societal norms, and contribute to conversations and movements for positive change. Sharing your artistic journey also lets you document your growth and progression. It becomes a record of your creative development and a testament to your artistic legacy. It allows others, including future generations, to understand your creative process, ideas, and contributions to the artistic landscape. However, the most important reason for sharing your art is the personal fulfillment it brings. Sharing your artistic journey and creations can bring a deep sense of joy and satisfaction. It allows you to share a part of yourself, express your thoughts and emotions, and contribute to the world through your unique creative expression. Sharing can bring a sense of purpose, fulfillment, and joy as you witness your art's impact on others.

Despite these benefits, showing your work can be scary. There are also practical issues, such as how best to achieve this. We will deal with the latter issue first. So, how can you exhibit your art and connect with others through your work? Local art galleries and exhibition spaces are a great starting point. Research local venues that showcase emerging artists or provide opportunities for beginners. Reach out to these galleries and inquire about exhibiting your work. Many galleries have specific submission guidelines or open calls for artists to participate in group exhibitions. Art competitions and juried exhibitions are another avenue to explore. Look for events that are open to beginners or emerging artists. Participating in these events not only provides exposure for your work but also allows you to connect with other artists and gain recognition from art professionals. Many of these are online events, but it is a start. Art fairs and markets are also great for beginners to showcase their work. These events often attract a diverse audience interested in supporting local artists. Rent a booth or table to display your artwork, engage with visitors, and make sales or connections. In today's digital age, online platforms and social media play a significant role in showcasing art. Create a professional portfolio website or utilize art-specific platforms like Behance, DeviantArt, or ArtStation to display your artwork. Additionally, utilize social media platforms like Instagram, Facebook, or Twitter to share images of your artwork, connect with other artists, and engage with potential buyers or art enthusiasts. Collaborative exhibitions or group shows can also be a valuable opportunity for beginners. Seek opportunities to collaborate with other artists or participate in group shows. Collaborative exhibitions provide a supportive environment and allow you to leverage multiple artists' collective exposure and networks. Connect with local artist communities or art organizations to explore collaborative exhibition possibilities. Artist open calls and residencies are another avenue to consider. Keep an eye out for open calls and residency programs accessible to beginners. These opportunities provide dedicated time and space for artists to create and exhibit their work. Research local and national open calls and artist residencies that align with your artistic practice and goals. Artwork Archive has a listing service, for example, of residency programs. For those who prefer a more hands-on approach, organizing their own exhibition can be a rewarding experience. Your town or district may not have all of these opportunities, so you and your fellow artists need to create your own. There is nothing wrong with that. Find suitable venues such as community spaces, cafes, or even your own home, and curate your artwork collection to display. Invite friends, family, and members of your artistic community to attend the exhibition. As we have explored, sharing your creativity brings joy and fulfillment in various ways. When you share your work, you open yourself up to receiving validation and recognition from others. This validation can be deeply fulfilling and provide a sense of purpose and affirmation in your creative pursuits. Sharing your work also allows you to connect emotionally and intellectually with others. Art can evoke emotions, spark conversations, and create meaningful connections. When your work resonates with someone else, it establishes a shared experience and can positively impact their lives. Knowing that your art has touched someone or made a difference can be incredibly fulfilling and reinforces the value of your creative expression. Moreover, sharing your creativity allows you to express yourself authentically. It provides a platform to communicate your thoughts, emotions, and unique perspectives. Through sharing, you create an avenue for your voice to be heard, and that act of self-expression can bring a deep sense of fulfillment and satisfaction. Sharing your work also opens doors for growth and learning as an artist. Feedback from others, whether it's constructive criticism or supportive comments, can offer valuable insights and perspectives. Engaging with an audience can push you to explore new ideas, experiment with different techniques, and continuously develop your artistic skills. Sharing and receiving feedback becomes a catalyst for growth and improvement, leading to a sense of personal fulfillment.

What if this entire idea scares you?

By now, you know this simply stems from fear in your past experiences. You want to avoid being hurt or embarrassed. Totally normal. However, you know that this fear is holding you back. You need to overcome this issue. Overcoming self-limiting fears and taking the first steps to show your work as a beginner artist can be challenging but immensely rewarding. Here are some strategies to help you overcome these fears:

1. Start Small and Safe. Begin by sharing your work with a supportive group of friends, family, or fellow artists. Choose people who you know will provide constructive and encouraging feedback. Host a small art show at your home or share your work on a private social media group. This creates a safe environment for initial exposure.

2. Seek Constructive Criticism. Understand that constructive criticism is an essential part of artistic growth. Seek feedback from those who can provide valuable insights to help you improve. Join online communities like DeviantArt, ArtStation, or local art groups where you can share your work and receive constructive feedback.

3. Focus on Progress, Not Perfection. Shift your mindset from seeking perfection to celebrating progress. Remember that every artist starts as a beginner and that improvement comes with practice. Keep a visual diary or portfolio of your work to track your progress over time. This helps you see how far you've come and reinforces the idea that growth is a journey.

4. Build Confidence Through Practice. The more you create and share, the more confident you will become. Regular practice helps you get comfortable with the process of making and showing art. Set aside dedicated time each day or week for your art practice. Share your work regularly, starting with smaller platforms before moving to larger, more public venues.

5. Embrace Rejection as Part of the Process. Understand that not everyone will appreciate your work, and that's okay. Rejection is a natural part of any creative journey and can be a stepping stone to improvement. Reframe rejection as an opportunity to learn and grow. Each piece of feedback is a chance to refine your skills and develop resilience.

Practical Steps to Get Started:

1. Create an Online Portfolio: Use platforms like Instagram, Behance, or your own website to showcase your work. These platforms allow you to reach a broader audience and receive feedback in a controlled way.

2. Participate in Art Challenges: Join online art challenges or prompts (e.g., Inktober, Draw This In Your Style) to motivate yourself to create and share regularly. These communities are often supportive and provide a sense of camaraderie.

3. Attend Art Classes or Workshops: Enroll in local or online art classes where you can share your work with peers. The structured environment can help reduce anxiety about sharing your work.

4. Submit to Local Art Shows or Galleries: Look for local opportunities to display your work, such as community centers, cafes, or art fairs. These venues are often welcoming to beginners and provide great exposure.

5. Network with Other Artists: Build relationships with other artists who can offer support, advice, and encouragement. Networking can also open up more opportunities to display your work.

Remember, the journey of showing your art is as important as the destination. Each step you take, no matter how small, helps you build confidence and resilience. By starting small, seeking supportive feedback, focusing on progress, practicing regularly, and embracing rejection as part of the process, you can overcome your fears and share your unique artistic voice with the world.

Art as a Legacy: Leaving Your Mark on the World

Art has the power to leave a lasting impact on the world, creating a legacy that extends far beyond your lifetime. Through art, you can shape and contribute to society's cultural landscape, inspire future generations, preserve memories and stories, impact social change, foster emotional connection and reflection, and provide aesthetic appreciation. Creating art with intention and purpose allows you to leave a mark on the world that reflects your unique perspective, ideas, and artistic voice. If changing the world is not in your plans, consider how your art can touch the lives of your friends and family. Inspire your grandchildren or leave profound memories for your children. This is all part of a legacy that is both emotional and tangible. Leaving a positive legacy through art requires thoughtful consideration and intentional action. Artists can start by defining their vision and values, clarifying the impact they want to make and the messages they want to convey through their art. Choosing meaningful themes and subjects that resonate with their vision and values allows artists to address social issues, promote empathy, and inspire positive change. Infusing positivity and inspiration into artwork is another way to leave a positive legacy. By creating art that uplifts and brings joy to viewers, you can instill a sense of optimism and beauty in your work. Using colors, symbols, and imagery that evoke positive emotions and convey optimism can profoundly impact the hearts and minds of those who encounter the art. I still recall a collector looking at one of my paintings. It was a scene with sunlight falling across a landscape. Rays of sunlight falling through the clouds created a warm and colorful landscape painting. However, to this viewer, it reminded him of his late mother. He became visibly emotional in my gallery and did not hesitate to purchase the painting. We can never underestimate the power of art. Fostering connection and empathy through art is also crucial in leaving a positive legacy. Artists can seek to understand and represent diverse perspectives and experiences, encouraging viewers to reflect on their own lives and connect with the emotions and stories portrayed in the artwork. Art can bridge divides, promote understanding, and nurture a sense of unity by fostering empathy. Educating and inspiring others is another practical way to leave a positive legacy through art. Artists can share their artistic knowledge, skills, and techniques with others, mentoring aspiring artists, teaching workshops, or contributing to educational programs that promote art and creativity. By sharing their expertise, artists can inspire and empower others to explore their artistic paths and make a positive impact through their creative endeavors. Documenting and archiving artwork is essential in preserving an artistic legacy. You can establish a system for documenting and archiving your artwork and creative process, maintaining a comprehensive record that ensures the preservation of your artistic legacy. This documentation facilitates future exhibitions, publications, or research on their artistic contributions. I like using Artwork Archive as a digital record system online. Also, consider storing digital records on a cloud storage system as a backup to your external hard drive. Keep your physical art safe, clean, and, if necessary, insured by describing it in your insurance contract.

It should go without saying, that you need to sign your art clearly. Describe the scene or name the painting adequately on the rear of the painting. These steps can be helpful to your family. Indeed, one day, it may be vital for the provenance of your work. Collaborating and engaging with communities is another practical way to leave a positive legacy through art. Artists can seek opportunities to collaborate with other artists, organizations, or communities, participating in group exhibitions, community art projects, or public art initiatives. Engaging with others allows for exchanging ideas, perspectives, and skills, strengthening the impact and reach of artistic endeavors. Regular reflection on the artistic journey and the impact being made is crucial in leaving a positive legacy through art. Artists should evaluate how their art aligns with their vision and values, considering how they can continually evolve and improve their creative practice to create a more meaningful and positive legacy. Reflective practice ensures that art remains purposeful and connected to the desired impact. Actively sharing art through various channels and platforms is another practical way to leave a positive legacy. Artists can utilize social media, personal websites, exhibitions, publications, and collaborations to extend the reach of their work. Seeking opportunities to engage with diverse audiences and communities allows art to have a broader impact and leave a positive legacy. Leaving a positive artistic legacy is an ongoing process that requires dedication, intention, and reflection. By incorporating art into your life and engaging with your community, you can create a positive artistic legacy that enriches the lives of others and leaves a lasting impact on the world.

The Art of Rest: Knowing When to Pause in Your Creative Journey

As a motivated creative, you pour your heart and soul into your work, striving for mastery and a sense of purpose. Dedication to your craft is commendable and often serves as a powerful antidote to destructive patterns and aimlessness. However, there are moments when even the most passionate artists need to take a step back and recharge. Understanding when and how to rest is crucial for maintaining your creative vitality. This chapter explores the importance of taking breaks, offering advice on how to rest effectively and return stronger.

It's important to recognize when you need a break. Creative fatigue can set in, leaving you feeling disaffected and uninspired. This isn't a sign of laziness; it's your mind and body signaling a need to regroup. Pushing through this fatigue can lead to burnout, stifling your creativity and diminishing your passion for your work.

To identify when you need a break, pay attention to these signs:

- **Loss of Inspiration:** When ideas stop flowing and you feel stuck, it might be time to step back.

- **Physical Exhaustion:** Creativity requires energy. If you're feeling physically drained, your creative output will suffer.

- **Mental Fatigue:** Difficulty focusing, constant frustration, and a lack of enthusiasm are indicators that your mental batteries need recharging.

- **Emotional Disconnection:** If you find yourself disconnected from your work emotionally, it's a clear sign that you need to rest and reset.

The Benefits of Taking a Break

Taking a break from your creative work can provide numerous benefits:

- **Mental Recharge:** Stepping away allows your mind to rest and rejuvenate, leading to renewed clarity and focus.

- **Enhanced Creativity:** Breaks give your subconscious time to mull over ideas, often leading to fresh insights and innovative solutions.

- **Improved Well-being:** Resting helps reduce stress and prevent burnout, ensuring you maintain a healthy relationship with your creative pursuits.

- **Balanced Perspective:** Time away from your work can provide new perspectives, helping you approach your projects with a refreshed mindset.

Effective Ways to Rest and Recharge

When it's time to take a break, consider these strategies to ensure you rest effectively:

- **Disconnect:** Step away from your workspace and disconnect from your projects. Engage in activities unrelated to your creative work, such as reading, walking, or spending time with loved ones.

- **Engage in Physical Activity:** Exercise can be a great way to clear your mind and recharge your energy levels. Activities like yoga, hiking, or swimming can help you feel rejuvenated.

- **Walking:** Spending quiet time in nature can help calm your mind and reduce stress.

- **Pursue Hobbies:** Engage in hobbies that you enjoy but differ from your primary creative work. This can provide a refreshing change of pace and stimulate your creativity in new ways.

- **Allow for Downtime:** Sometimes, doing nothing is the best way to recharge. Allow yourself to rest without guilt, understanding that this downtime is essential for your overall well-being and future creative productivity.

Returning to Your Creative Work

After taking a break, you'll likely return to your creative work with renewed energy and enthusiasm. Here are some tips for re-engaging with your projects:

- **Ease Back In.** Start with small tasks to gradually get back into your workflow. I like to prime painting panels and tone them with a color to prepare them for painting.

- **Set New Goals:** Use the clarity gained during your break to set fresh, achievable goals for your creative projects.

- **Reflect on Your Rest:** Consider what aspects of your break were most rejuvenating and how to incorporate regular, shorter breaks into your routine.

- **Stay Flexible:** Remember that you are your own freelancer. Maintain flexibility in your schedule to accommodate future breaks when needed.

Always make time for your loved ones.

Make sure you connect with your significant other. My wife and I always meet up during the day for tea, lunch, and a sundowner. Yes, we are working in the same building but doing our own creative pursuits. We can become blocked and stressed if we do not sit down and chat about them. Talking over a cuppa is a mini-rest. It also keeps us connected. Make time for your children. I enjoy walking the dogs and will have my children walk with me. We talk or enjoy the walk in the fresh air. In whatever form these breaks make sense for you, take them often. Remember, you are not a slave to your work but a freelancer in control of your creative journey. So kick off your shoes, relax, and give yourself the gift of rest. Your creative spirit will thank you.

Embracing the Present: Creativity and Self-Awareness as Antidotes to the Illusion of Greener Pastures

In our hyperconnected world, the temptation to constantly seek greener pastures can overshadow the blessings of our present moment. The relentless comparison driven by social media and the desire for a better, more glamorous life often leaves us feeling unfulfilled despite our many fortunes. This chapter explores how cultivating creativity and self-awareness can liberate us from this cycle of discontent, enabling us to embrace the present with gratitude and authenticity.

The saying "the grass is always greener on the other side" encapsulates a common human experience: the belief that others have it better than we do and that happiness lies just out of reach. This mindset is perpetuated by the constant barrage of curated perfection on social media, where everyone else seems to be living their best lives, free from struggles or imperfections. Can you relate to this? I am sorry to say that I have also had these moments. Seeing a school friend, for example, posting about their great success can create a jealous moment. Terrible. One of our less admirable human qualities.

Creativity offers a powerful antidote to this illusion. When you engage in creative activities, you enter a state of flow where time loses grip, and you are fully present in the moment. Creativity allows you to connect with your true self, free from external comparisons, whether painting, writing, sculpting, or playing music. This immersion in the creative process fosters a deep sense of fulfillment and contentment as you find joy in the act of creation itself.

Self-awareness involves a mindful examination of your thoughts, feelings, and motivations. By becoming more aware of your inner landscape, you can identify the sources of your discontent and recognize the patterns of comparison that fuel your desire for greener pastures. This awareness allows you to challenge and replace these thoughts with a more grounded and appreciative mindset. You will understand that no matter where you end up, there you are. The same confused and self-absorbed person. Until you see the truth and remove the illusions of what success looks like.

Practicing gratitude is a key component of self-awareness. Regularly reflecting on the positive aspects of your life shifts your focus from what you lack to what you have. This shift in perspective can transform your outlook, helping you to see the richness of your current circumstances and reducing the allure of the illusory greener pastures.

Imagine yourself twenty years from now, looking back on your life today. What would you give to be back in this moment, with its unique opportunities and experiences? This thought experiment can be a powerful motivator to appreciate the present. It underscores the transient nature of time and the importance of living fully in the now rather than pining for a different reality.

While it's important to aspire for growth and improvement, living your best life in the present is equally crucial. This means taking care of your physical health through a balanced diet and regular exercise and nurturing your mental and emotional well-being through creativity and mindful living. By focusing on what you love and engaging deeply in these activities, you create a life that is rich, fulfilling, and authentically yours. Above all, you will become awake to your life in the many forms described in this book.

Let Go of the Past and Make a New Beginning

The creative awakening is not a destination but a lifelong journey. It is a commitment to continuous growth, exploration, and self-discovery. Our perspectives, experiences, and values evolve throughout our lives, and our creative awakening involves embracing these changes and allowing them to influence our artistic expression. Our creative voice evolves and deepens as we gain new insights and explore different aspects of ourselves and the world. Creativity is a dynamic and ever-expanding realm; there is always something new to learn. Whether exploring different artistic techniques, experimenting with various mediums, or delving into unfamiliar subjects, lifelong learning keeps our creativity fresh and inspires us to push boundaries. Through this learning and exploration process, we find inner peace and fulfillment. Creativity thrives in the realm of the unknown. It requires stepping outside our comfort zones, taking risks, and embracing uncertainty. A lifelong commitment to creative awakening means continually challenging ourselves, seeking new experiences, and exploring uncharted territories within our artistic practice. Through this embrace of the unknown, we find the true essence of our creativity. We must understand that holding onto the past will not help in this journey forward. So many people are hindered by their past because they do not want to let go. Even a painful past feels safer and more familiar than the new path. Acknowledging the past and then letting it recede. Move onwards and create a new world in the present. The creative journey often entails challenges, setbacks, and moments of self-doubt. But a lifelong commitment to creative awakening means developing resilience and perseverance. It involves pushing through obstacles, learning from failures, and maintaining the dedication to continue creating despite difficulties. Through these moments of resilience, we find the strength to overcome and grow. Creative awakening is a path of self-discovery. It invites us to delve into our innermost thoughts, emotions, and experiences. This process is ongoing as we uncover new layers of ourselves throughout life. By engaging in creative expression, we tap into our subconscious, gain insights into our true selves, and deepen our understanding of our complexities. Creativity is intertwined with personal growth and transformation. It involves embracing change, shedding old limitations, and allowing ourselves to evolve as artists and individuals. Through our creative practice, we explore our identities, challenge assumptions, and cultivate a greater sense of authenticity and purpose. Through this process of growth and transformation, we find the true essence of our creative selves. Creativity is a powerful connector. A lifelong commitment to creative awakening provides opportunities to connect with like-minded individuals, collaborate with other artists, and share our work with a broader community. These connections enrich our creative journey, inspire us, and provide invaluable support and feedback. Through these connections, we find the strength and encouragement to continue on our creative path. For those who are hesitant or keep putting off their artistic endeavors, there are ways to take the initiative and start creating. Starting small is key, breaking down creative goals into smaller, manageable steps. Embracing imperfection is crucial, releasing the need for perfection and embracing the joy of the creative process. Making art a priority by dedicating time specifically for creative pursuits and creating accountability by sharing goals with others can also help continue the creative journey. Setting realistic expectations, experimenting and exploring different mediums, finding inspiration, and overcoming resistance are all important steps in continuing to explore creativity and finding inner peace through art. Practicing self-compassion and enjoying the art creation process is also essential in sustaining a lifelong commitment to creative awakening. There are countless personal experiences and examples of individuals who have made art a central part of their lives for continued growth and fulfillment. From painters to writers, musicians to dancers, artists of all disciplines have found solace, joy, and a sense of purpose through their creative pursuits. Pick your favorite celebrity artist and read their biography. You will see that all these famous people had to overcome adversity. Their stories serve as inspiration and a testament to the transformative power of art. Making art a lifelong pursuit comes with numerous benefits. It nourishes the soul, brings mental and emotional well-being, fosters personal growth and development, allows for unique expression and perspective, inspires and connects with others, and leaves a lasting legacy and impact. Individuals can find fulfillment, purpose, and inner peace by prioritizing art and embracing the creative awakening as a new beginning.

Activities and Ideas for Healing Through Art

In this chapter, let us consider the transformative power of healing art practices. These creative activities can remarkably promote physical, emotional, and mental well-being. Engaging in these practices can help individuals find solace, reduce stress levels, and cultivate inner peace. Let us explore some of the most potent healing art practices that have captured the imagination of professionals and enthusiasts alike. One such practice is Art Therapy. This therapeutic approach harnesses various art forms like painting, drawing, sculpture, and collage to provide a safe space for individuals to express their deepest thoughts, emotions, and experiences. Often utilized in clinical settings to address mental health issues or trauma-related challenges, Art Therapy has proven to be a powerful tool for self-discovery and healing. Another fascinating practice is Music Therapy. It utilizes the universal language of music to address physical ailments and emotional, cognitive, and social needs. Through activities like singing or playing instruments under the guidance of skilled therapists, individuals can experience improved mood states while simultaneously reducing anxiety levels. Harmonious notes pave the way for enhanced communication skills within oneself and with others. Dance/Movement Therapy offers a unique avenue for emotional expression through body movement and dance sequences. This awe-inspiring practice enables individuals to process deep-seated emotions effectively while cultivating heightened body awareness. As stress management becomes more important than ever before, Dance/Movement Therapy provides an innovative path toward holistic wellness. Writing Therapy or bibliotherapy allows individuals to embark on a journey of self-expression through writing endeavors. Journaling allows one's innermost thoughts to flow freely onto paper, while poetry serves as an outlet for creative exploration within oneself's emotional landscape. Narrative therapy empowers individuals by providing them with the tools necessary to explore their life stories while addressing any emotional challenges they may face along their narratives. Daily writing practice has many benefits, including getting your day more organized, your thoughts settled, and your concerns illuminated. The world of Drama Therapy embraces theatrical techniques such as role-playing and improvisation. Through these transformative activities, individuals gain the opportunity to explore and resolve emotional and psychological challenges. For those who find it easier to express themselves through acting, Drama Therapy becomes a gateway towards self-discovery and personal growth. With its intricate geometric designs within a circular shape, Mandala Creation offers a meditative practice for relaxation, self-discovery, and stress reduction. By drawing or coloring mandalas, individuals embark on a transformative journey that fosters inner harmony while providing an avenue for creative expression. The adult coloring book concept has proven to be more than a fad. It is fun and calming. It may also lead to your creative nature coming forward and assert itself. Photography invites individuals to capture and explore their emotions, experiences, and perspectives through images. The camera lens becomes a tool for self-reflection as one delves into the depth of one's being while allowing one's unique vision to shine through. Nature-Based Art Therapy encourages individuals to engage in creative activities outdoors in natural settings. Painting in a park or creating land art allows one to connect with nature profoundly while facilitating emotional healing and relaxation. Why not combine nature with painting outdoors? Clay and Pottery Therapy provides a tactile experience that grounds individuals while allowing them to sculpt and create three-dimensional art. This hands-on approach instills a sense of accomplishment as one molds clay into magnificent forms. Color Therapy, or Chromotherapy, uses specific colors to evoke emotional responses and psychological healing. Coloring books designed for adults have become popular as calming activities that effectively alleviate stress. Crafting and DIY Projects become therapeutic endeavors as they enable individuals to create something tangible with their own hands. Engaging in knitting, woodworking, or making jewelry fosters relaxation and an innate sense of achievement. The emergence of digital art has paved the way for Virtual Reality Therapy, an innovative medium that provides immersive experiences for creative expression and healing. These cutting-edge technologies unlock new dimensions where virtual worlds intertwine with reality, offering unique opportunities for personal growth. Participating in Community Art Projects provides an avenue for connection amidst diverse communities. Collaborating on mural paintings or public art installations fosters a sense of purpose and belonging while benefiting both individuals and the communities they serve. These healing art practices can be tailored to individual preferences and needs, making them versatile tools for personal growth and well-being. Whether integrated into therapeutic settings or utilized as self-help techniques, these activities hold immense potential for transformation. However, it is imperative to acknowledge that while these practices yield substantial benefits, they are not intended to replace professional medical or psychological treatment when necessary. In this ever-evolving world, where stressors seem omnipresent, embracing healing art practices can serve as an anchor amidst the chaos. By embarking on this creative journey towards inner peace and mindfulness, individuals unlock profound insights into their beings while nurturing their mental well-being. The power of art transcends boundaries - it heals wounds unseen, offering solace in the most unexpected places.

Teaching as a Way to Learn and Pay it Forward

Teaching art is not only a way to share your passion with others but also a powerful tool for personal growth and development. Whether you choose to teach in-person workshops, online courses, or collaborate with other teachers, teaching allows you to deepen your understanding of your craft while positively impacting others. When you teach art to groups, whether it's a local art society or an online community, you can connect with fellow artists who share your love for creativity. By sharing your knowledge and expertise, you are helping others improve their skills and fostering a sense of belonging within the artistic community. This exchange of ideas and techniques can spark inspiration and new perspectives that can further enhance your own artistic journey. Teaching art through platforms like YouTube or online courses provides accessibility to aspiring artists worldwide. Through these digital mediums, you can reach individuals who may not have access to traditional art education or resources in their local communities. By sharing your expertise through tutorials and demonstrations, you empower them to explore their creativity and develop their artistic abilities. I can confirm all of this is true. From Iceland to Australia, the variety of artists I have encountered through my art classes is astonishing. This is one of the positive achievements of our connected world. Why not use it to full advantage and grow as a person and in your skills? In addition to expanding your artistic horizons through teaching, there is also an immense sense of fulfillment that comes from giving back. By imparting your knowledge to others, you are contributing to the growth of the global art society. Each student you inspire becomes part of a ripple effect that spreads creativity and self-expression worldwide. Teaching art can be both financially rewarding and personally fulfilling. While paid classes compensate for your time and expertise, the true value lies in the connections formed with students as they grow artistically under your guidance. Witnessing their progress fuels a sense of pride in knowing you played a role in their creative journey. However, teaching does not always have to be about financial gain; offering free classes or volunteering in community art projects allows you to give back to your local community. These acts of generosity benefit others and nurture your own soul. Teaching becomes a selfless expression of the Art Spirit, where the joy of sharing supersedes any monetary considerations. Teaching art is a reciprocal process where both the teacher and students learn and grow together. You gain a deeper understanding of your craft as you guide others in their artistic exploration. Teaching challenges you to articulate concepts, break down techniques, and think critically about your artistic process. In turn, this enhanced understanding translates into personal growth as an artist. Moreover, teaching art forces you to expand your knowledge base continually. To effectively communicate complex ideas and techniques, you must stay updated with the latest trends and developments in the art world. This ongoing pursuit of knowledge keeps your artistic practice dynamic and ensures that you are constantly pushing yourself outside of your comfort zone. Teaching also cultivates essential skills such as communication, empathy, and patience. Each student has unique learning styles and abilities, so adapting your teaching methods to cater to their needs hones these interpersonal skills. These transferrable skills can be applied not only in the classroom but also in other areas of life. Embrace teaching as an integral part of your creative journey—an acceptance of the Art Spirit that transcends financial compensation and immerses you in the beauty of shared creativity.

Practical Steps to Creating Mindfully

The path to awakening our creative selves and living a life of mindful presence is not merely a theoretical exercise. It requires us to get our hands dirty, to step away from the digital distractions, and immerse ourselves in tangible experiences that engage our senses and challenge our minds. In this section, we will explore a variety of hands-on activities and practices that can help us cultivate a beginner's mind, embrace imperfection, and develop the lateral thinking skills necessary for true creative expression. From the art of handcrafting to the joy of gardening, from mindful movement to the power of play, we will delve into practical ways to unplug from distractions, reconnect with ourselves and our surroundings, and tap into the wellspring of creativity within each of us. These exercises are not mere diversions; they are pathways to personal growth, problem-solving prowess, and a deeper appreciation for the beauty and wonder surrounding us when we approach life with open eyes, minds, and hearts.

If you are already deep into your creative activity, then you may be ready to dabble in something different. I do not mean stop your main activity, but be present with some other activity. For example, I like getting into the garden and doing a few DIY projects. This keeps me hands-on and makes a positive impact on our home life.

What practical activities can you do today to give yourself a mini-break from art? How about cooking, baking, or setting up a gourmet barbecue for the family? The only condition is that it must be hands-on and contribute in some way to your quality of life.

A creative solution to the cluttered and grubby garage? Make it a project to transform that space into a welcoming one. Is the garden path looking untidy? Fix it with flair. Does the front door need a lick of paint? Make it something special that welcomes you each day.

Now is the time to make a change for the better.

Perfectionism is the Hurdle: How to Overcome this Self-Sabotage

For perfectionists and those who struggle with self-sabotage, pursuing flawlessness can become an insurmountable barrier to creative expression and personal growth. However, by embracing the principles of wabi-sabi—the Japanese worldview that finds beauty in imperfection, impermanence, and incompleteness—we can learn to let go of the need for perfection and find liberation in the unfinished.

Do you know someone like this? Is it you or a loved one? I see this in a family member. She is so talented but carries baggage from her school days. The need to create perfect work is so strong that she often stops before the work is complete. This is a protection mechanism where the ego finds an excuse or rationalization to drop the project. This is pure fear. Irrational fear. She would rather avoid the pleasure of completing a project to avoid the *imagined* pain of being embarrassed with less-than-perfect work. Sad, but quite common too.

Here are some practical techniques that can help both perfectionists and those prone to self-sabotage overcome their triggers and embrace the beauty of imperfection:

1. Reframe your mindset: Challenge the notion that imperfection is a flaw or a failure. Instead, view imperfections as unique markers of authenticity, individuality, and the human touch. Appreciate the character and charm that imperfections can lend to your creative work.
2. Practice mindfulness: Engage in exercises that cultivate present-moment awareness and non-judgmental observation. When you notice yourself fixating on perceived flaws or doubting your abilities, gently bring your attention back to the present moment and the creation process itself.
3. Celebrate the journey: Shift your focus from the end result to the journey of creating. Find joy and fulfillment in exploration, experimentation, and self-expression rather than solely valuing the

final product.

4. Embrace the art of wabi-sabi: Study examples of wabi-sabi in art, design, and nature. Observe the beauty in worn textures, asymmetry, and the patina of age. Allow these perspectives to inform your own artistic practice and help you appreciate the imperfect and unfinished.

5. Set realistic goals: Instead of striving for unattainable perfection, set achievable, incremental goals for your creative projects. Break larger tasks into smaller, manageable steps, and celebrate each milestone along the way.

6. Practice self-compassion: Be kind and understanding towards yourself when faced with setbacks or perceived failures. Recognize that self-criticism and harsh self-judgment only perpetuate the cycle of self-sabotage and hinder your creative growth.

7. Seek support: Surround yourself with a supportive community of fellow artists who understand the challenges of embracing imperfection. Share your struggles openly, and learn from the experiences and perspectives of others on similar journeys.

8. Explore the roots: For those whose perfectionism or self-sabotage stems from deep-rooted childhood experiences, consider seeking professional guidance or therapy. Understanding the root causes can help you develop coping strategies and break free from limiting patterns.

Remember, the journey towards creative awakening is not about achieving flawlessness but about embracing the beauty of the imperfect, the unfinished, and the ever-evolving nature of the creative process. By learning to let go of the need for perfection, you can unlock a sense of freedom, authenticity, and joy in your artistic endeavors.

Cultivating a Beginner's Mind: Embracing Curiosity and Lifelong Learning

Be Open to Lifelong Learning Yet Remain Humble in Wisdom

As artists, it's all too easy to fall into the trap of complacency, relying on familiar techniques and methods that have served us well in the past. However, true creativity thrives when we approach our craft with a beginner's mind – a state of openness, curiosity, and a willingness to accept the unknown. While I was still practicing as an attorney, the Law Society had a continuous learning system. Attorneys had to attend several seminars yearly to brush up on new developments. Sometimes, this could be a nuisance, but I knew keeping up with the new laws was important. Now, you need to bring that mindset to your art and creative pursuits. Also, your business and marketing skills if you have gone down that route too.

Hopefully, this is fun for you, but in case you are finding it difficult to develop the learning habit, here are some practical tips to help you cultivate a beginner's mind and foster a spirit of perpetual curiosity and lifelong learning:

1. Seek out new experiences: Step out of your comfort zone and immerse yourself in activities or environments that are unfamiliar to you. Whether it's taking a class in a different artistic medium, exploring a new cultural tradition, or simply venturing into a part of town you've never visited before, new experiences have a way of sparking fresh perspectives and inspiring creative growth.

2. Ask questions: Don't be afraid to approach your craft with the inquisitive mindset of a child. Question your assumptions, challenge your preconceptions, and seek out new knowledge and insights from mentors, peers, or even those outside your artistic circle. Embrace the idea that there is always more to learn, and approach each new lesson with humility and wonder.

3. Experiment without fear: Give yourself permission to play and experiment without the pressure of perfection. Set aside dedicated time for creative exploration, where the only goal is to try new techniques, materials, or approaches without judging the outcome. Embrace the possibility of "failure" as an opportunity for growth and discovery.

4. Observe with fresh eyes: Make a conscious effort to observe the world around you with heightened awareness and curiosity. Study the intricate details of nature, the interplay of light and shadow, or the nuances of human behavior. You'll cultivate a wellspring of inspiration and insight by training your eye to see the extraordinary in the ordinary.

5. Seek diverse perspectives: Surround yourself with individuals from diverse backgrounds, disciplines, and viewpoints. Engage in thoughtful discussions, attend lectures or workshops outside your usual realm, and actively seek perspectives that challenge your own. This cross-pollination of ideas can spark new ways of thinking and fuel your creative growth.

6. Embrace beginner's mind: Approach each new project, each new challenge, with the mindset of a beginner – free from preconceptions and open to the possibilities that lie ahead. Cultivate a sense of wonder and humility, allowing yourself to be guided by curiosity and a willingness to learn.

By embracing these practices, you'll keep your artistic spark alive and cultivate a deeper appreciation for the journey of lifelong learning and creative exploration. Remember, it's not about mastering a fixed set of skills; it's about embracing the ever-evolving process of growth, discovery, and creative awakening.

A note of caution, though.

Remaining humble and avoiding the pitfalls of arrogance or a "know-it-all" attitude is crucial when cultivating a beginner's mind and embracing lifelong learning. Here's how we could incorporate that idea:

7. Maintain humility: While seeking out diverse perspectives and continually expanding your knowledge is important, it's equally vital to maintain a sense of

humility. Remember that true wisdom lies in recognizing how much we have yet to learn. Approach new ideas and experiences with an open mind, free from the arrogance of assuming you already have all the answers. Nobody likes a know-it-all, so stay grounded, humble, and receptive to the lessons that life and others have to offer.

8. Celebrate wisdom, not bravado: True wisdom is not about flaunting your accomplishments or knowledge but rather about quiet confidence from a deep understanding of your craft and recognizing the vastness of what remains to be explored. Seek to embody this wisdom through your actions, your openness to learning, and your respect for the journeys of others.

By remaining humble yet wise, you'll create an environment conducive to growth, where curiosity can flourish and true creativity can take root. Remember, the path of lifelong learning is one of humility, wonder, and a willingness to embrace the fact that there will always be more to discover, experience, and explore.

Mindful Movement: Engaging the Body for Mental Clarity and Focus

Physical movement and exercise are essential to the creative awakening process, as they profoundly impact our mental and physical well-being. For the sedentary artist, cultivating a more holistic lifestyle incorporating regular physical activity can unlock new creative energy levels, mental clarity, and overall vitality.

Here's why movement and physical fitness are so important for creative awakening:

1. Increased oxygen flow and neurogenesis: Exercise increases blood flow and oxygen delivery to the brain, promoting the growth of new brain cells (neurogenesis) in areas associated with learning, memory, and overall cognitive function. As I get older, I become more aware of how important this topic is. I am also caring for elderly parents, and this has rammed home the consequences of too much time being seated and not enough muscle strength.

2. Stress reduction and emotional regulation: Regular physical activity has been shown to reduce stress levels, anxiety, and depression, all of which can be significant barriers to creativity. Exercise helps regulate emotions and promote a sense of calm and clarity.

3. Enhanced focus and concentration: Mindful movement practices, such as yoga or tai chi, can improve our ability to stay present, focused, and attentive, which is crucial for creative work that requires sustained concentration.

4. Boosted energy and stamina: Regular exercise increases overall energy levels, endurance, and stamina, providing the physical vitality necessary to sustain long periods of creative endeavors.

Here are some practical tips to help sedentary artists incorporate physical exercise into their creative process. Remember to consult your doctor if you have any potential physical conditions that may be adversely affected by exercise. Common sense comes first.

1. Start small and build consistency: Begin with manageable goals, such as taking a daily 20-minute walk or doing a short yoga sequence in the morning. Consistency is key; even small amounts of regular movement can yield significant benefits. What helps me get outdoors twice a day is having energetic dogs. Walking them is a necessity that has become a pleasure for me. My fitness improved, and I get all the benefits of exercise and awareness of my surroundings.

2. Embrace mindful movement practices: Explore mindful practices like yoga, tai chi, or qigong, which combine physical movement with breath work and present-moment awareness, fostering a deeper mind-body connection.

3. Incorporate movement breaks: During extended periods of creative work, set reminders to take short movement breaks every hour or so. Stretch, light calisthenics, or walk around for a few minutes to rejuvenate your body and mind.

4. Explore outdoor activities: Engage in outdoor activities like hiking, cycling, or gardening, which not only provide physical exercise but also allow you to connect with nature, a potent source of creative inspiration.

5. Find activities you enjoy: Experiment with different forms of exercise until you find activities that resonate with you and bring you joy and fulfillment. When movement is pleasurable, it becomes a sustainable part of your lifestyle.

Remember, the goal is not to become a professional athlete but to cultivate a balanced, holistic approach to your creative practice. By engaging in mindful movement and prioritizing physical fitness, you'll unlock new reserves of energy, clarity, and creative potential, allowing you to fully embrace the journey of awakening your artistic self.

Gardening as a Metaphor for Life: Nurturing Growth and Embracing Change

Gardening is a profoundly grounding and therapeutic activity that can benefit artists physically and mentally. Beyond the obvious physical exercise involved in tending to a garden, nurturing living plants serves as a powerful metaphor for the creative process itself—a journey of patience, nurturing growth, and embracing change.

For the active and fit artist, the physical labor of creating and maintaining a backyard garden can be an invigorating experience. Digging, weeding, and tilling the soil provide a full-body workout, while the repetitive motions of pruning and planting can induce a meditative state, allowing the mind to wander and sparking creative insights. Consider a kitchen garden that rewards you with herbs. Not only does this make your food healthier and tastier, but you also have a sense of satisfaction.

"I grew a thing!" is an exclamation I overuse, but it makes me laugh.

However, gardening can still be a rewarding and restorative pursuit even for those with limited space or mobility. With the right approach, a balcony, windowsill, or even a small indoor space can be transformed into a verdant oasis.

Here are some tips for incorporating gardening into your creative practice, regardless of your physical abilities or living situation:

1. Container gardening: Grow a variety of herbs, vegetables, or flowers in portable containers, which can be placed on balconies, patios, or even indoors near a sunny window.
2. Vertical gardening: Utilize vertical space by installing wall-mounted planters, hanging baskets, or even repurposing old bookshelves or ladders as creative plant displays.
3. Indoor gardening: Cultivate low-maintenance houseplants or even create a miniature indoor garden with a terrarium or a hydroponic

system, allowing you to nurture greenery year-round.

4. Community gardening: If you lack outdoor space, explore community gardens in your area, where you can rent a plot and connect with fellow gardeners, fostering a sense of community and shared knowledge.

5. Mindful gardening practices: Incorporate mindfulness into your gardening routine by focusing on the sensory experiences – the rich scents, the textures of soil and leaves, and the sounds of nature surrounding you. This heightened awareness can deepen your connection to the creative process.

For older individuals or those with mobility challenges, raised garden beds or elevated planters can alleviate the need for excessive bending or kneeling. At the same time, ergonomic tools can make gardening tasks more comfortable and accessible.

Beyond the physical benefits, gardening is a powerful metaphor for the creative journey. Just as a gardener must nurture seedlings with patience and care, an artist must tend to their creative ideas, allowing them to grow and evolve. And just as a garden embraces the natural cycles of change and renewal, artists must learn to embrace the ever-shifting nature of their craft, adapting and flourishing in the face of challenges and transitions.

By incorporating gardening into their lives, artists can cultivate a deeper appreciation for the interconnectedness of all living things, the beauty of imperfection, and the resilience inherent in the natural world – lessons that can profoundly enrich their creative endeavors and awaken a profound sense of wonder and gratitude.

Spending a little time in the garden can help me overcome frustration and anger. Sometimes, I need to get out of the studio and do something different, let off a bit of steam. Gardening for an hour will restore my sense of balance and calm my soul.

Building a Creative Community: Fostering Collaboration and Shared Growth

While the creative journey is often perceived as a solitary pursuit, the truth is that we all thrive when we have a supportive community to connect with, share ideas, and foster mutual growth. However, navigating the dynamics of a creative community can be challenging, especially when you have a diverse mix of personality types, from outgoing extroverts to more introspective introverts.

My personality is … you guessed it! I am an introvert by nature. This does not mean that I avoid people, either. It means I have to interact in a way that does not leave me exhausted. Smaller groups, more intimate workshops, and calmer environments work for me—not the grand stage. The internet also works for me. There are options for all types these days.

Here are some strategies that can help foster a vibrant, inclusive, creative community catering to extroverts and introverts. These tips are geared toward the artist who wants to build a community, whether for business or a non-profit meet-up group.

1. Offer various engagement options: Provide opportunities for social interaction and solitary pursuits within your community. Host group events like artist talks, workshops, or open studio nights, but also offer quieter spaces or virtual platforms where introverts can connect and share their work at their own pace.
2. Create structured and unstructured spaces: While extroverts may thrive in unstructured, spontaneous social settings, introverts often prefer more structured environments to prepare and feel comfortable. Offer a mix of both structured activities (like guided workshops or critiques) and unstructured social gatherings (like potlucks or casual meetups).
3. Encourage one-on-one connections: Facilitate opportunities for artists to connect more intimately, one-on-one. Implement a mentorship program, arrange studio visits, or organize small group critiques. These more personal interactions can be less overwhelming

for introverts while allowing for meaningful connections.

4. Foster online communities: Leverage digital platforms and social media to create virtual creative communities. Online forums, discussion groups, or even video conferencing sessions can provide a comfortable space for introverts to engage without the pressure of face-to-face interaction while still allowing for collaboration and idea sharing.

5. Respect personal boundaries: Emphasize the importance of respecting each individual's boundaries and comfort levels. Encourage open communication about preferences and needs, and create a culture of understanding and acceptance, where both extroverts and introverts feel valued and supported.

6. Lead by example: As a community leader or facilitator, model the behavior you wish to cultivate. Be mindful of creating a welcoming atmosphere, actively listening to diverse perspectives, and encouraging respectful dialogue, regardless of personality type.

7. Celebrate diverse contributions: Recognize that extroverts and introverts bring valuable strengths to the creative community. Appreciate the energy and enthusiasm of extroverts while also honoring the deep thinking and introspection of introverts. Foster an environment where all contributions are valued and celebrated.

By implementing these strategies, you can create an inclusive and nurturing creative community that celebrates diversity, fosters collaboration, and provides a supportive environment for artists of all personality types to thrive, grow, and awaken their creative potential. Start small and grow from there. One of my proudest achievements is my own live channel community[1] It is small yet filled with active and happy artists. I get a kick out of seeing how members have improved in their painting. It is super rewarding to make a difference in these artists' lives, even a small one. I know they enjoy it, and that is very satisfying.

---

1. https://malcolmdeweyfineart.newzenler.com/courses/artists-live-membership

The Power of Play: Rediscovering Childlike Wonder and Creativity

Is it too late?

For those trapped in the grind of a thankless desk job or facing retirement, rediscovering the art of play and tapping into their childlike sense of wonder can be a transformative experience. Are you burdened by the weight of perfectionism or the loss of your creative spark? If so, the power of play offers a path to awakening the joy and freedom that often elude us in adulthood.

Oh, are you tempted to dismiss this chapter as silly? If so, consider that other casualty of the all-too-serious life: the ability to laugh. When last did you have a good belly laugh? Not the polite laugh of civil society. I mean a good laugh from the soul. Too long? If this is not tragic enough, then consider that there are numerous health studies linking how important laughter is to keeping the little gray cells working into old age. So, let's have some fun!

Here are some practical strategies to help you reignite your playful spirits:

1. Identify and confront limiting beliefs: Begin by recognizing and challenging the limiting beliefs and self-imposed barriers that may stifle your ability to play. Question the notion that play is frivolous or unproductive, and remind yourself that play is essential for creativity, problem-solving, and overall well-being. Want to know a secret? I still have the yo-yo I played with as a child on my desk. I still have the skills, too!

2. Engage in nostalgia: Revisit the activities, games, and hobbies that brought you joy as a child. Whether coloring, building with Legos, or playing catch, these familiar pastimes can serve as gateways to recapturing that sense of carefree wonder and imagination. A little-known fact is that I used to be part of the yo-yo competitions in my town when I was a child. I still have a few of the "Genuine Russell Yo-Yos on my desk. Guess what? I am still pretty good, too.

3. Explore new realms of play: Step out of your comfort zone and try

something entirely new and whimsical. Learn some magic tricks, learn to juggle, or attend a painting party. Sip and paint, anyone? Engaging in novel activities can help break down inhibitions and reignite your playful spirit.

4. Embrace the silly and absurd: Allow yourself to be silly, goofy, and even slightly absurd. Laugh at yourself, make up silly songs or dances, and let go of the need always to be serious or "proper." This playful abandon can be incredibly liberating.

5. Play with others: Seek opportunities to play with friends and family or join a community of like-minded individuals who value play and creativity. Playing with others can help create a supportive environment and foster a sense of connection and shared joy.

6. Integrate play into your daily routine: Rather than relegating play to isolated events, find ways to weave playful elements into your daily life. Take a silly detour on your daily walk, experiment with new recipes in the kitchen, or turn mundane chores into games or challenges.

7. Celebrate the process, not the product: When engaging in playful activities, shift your focus away from the end result and instead savor the process itself. Embrace the freedom of exploration, experimentation, and self-expression without the pressure of perfection. Change up your wardrobe to give yourself a little more color. Change the frames of your glasses from dull corporate style to funky artist. Experiment.

8. Seek inspiration from children: Observe how children approach play with unbridled enthusiasm, curiosity, and imagination. Learn from their ability to fully immerse themselves in the present moment and find joy in the simplest of activities.

By embracing these strategies, those who have been weighed down by the demands of adulthood or the pursuit of perfection can rediscover the transformative power of play. Through play, they can reignite their creative spark, cultivate a sense of wonder and joy, and ultimately awaken to a more fulfilling and authentic expression of their true selves.

The Creative Genius Within: Unleashing Your Innate Problem-Solving Abilities

The Bonus

Unleashing our innate creative genius is not just about artistic expression or creative pursuits; it's also about cultivating a mindset and developing skills that enhance our problem-solving abilities, build our confidence, and help us approach life's challenges with a more centered and considered approach.

Within each of us lies an inherent creative genius – a wellspring of innovative thinking, resourcefulness, and problem-solving prowess waiting to be tapped. By awakening this inner genius, we not only unlock our artistic potential but also develop a powerful toolkit for navigating the complexities of life with greater ease and clarity.

One key benefit of unleashing our creative genius is the ability to approach problems from fresh perspectives. When we break free from rigid, conventional thinking patterns, we gain the flexibility to see challenges through new lenses, identify novel solutions, and make unexpected, overlooked connections.

Engaging our creative problem-solving abilities can help alleviate the overwhelm and anxiety often accompanying life's difficulties. Instead of succumbing to reactive, frantic responses, we learn to step back, thoughtfully consider various approaches, and trust our ability to find innovative solutions. As the adage goes, "Sleep on it, and the answer appears in the morning" – a testament to the power of allowing our subconscious creative genius to work its magic.

Cultivating this innate genius also fosters confidence and self-assurance. As we experience the satisfaction of successfully resolving challenges through our own creative insights, we develop a deeper belief in our capabilities and a greater sense of personal agency. This, in turn, can lead to a more centered and peaceful mindset, as we no longer feel overwhelmed by life's curveballs but rather empowered to tackle them head-on.

To unleash your creative genius and enhance your problem-solving abilities, consider the following practices:

1. Embrace curiosity: Approach challenges with curiosity and an eagerness to explore multiple perspectives. Ask questions, seek diverse viewpoints, and remain open to unexpected insights. Always take the approach of: "This can be solved."
2. Engage in divergent thinking: Practice generating many ideas, no matter how unconventional or seemingly unrelated. Suspend judgment and allow your mind to wander freely, making unexpected connections.
3. Experiment and iterate: Don't be afraid to try out potential solutions, even if they seem unconventional. Embrace a mindset of experimentation, iterating, and refining your ideas through hands-on exploration.
4. Cultivate mindfulness: Develop the ability to quiet your mind, observe your thoughts without judgment, and tap into your intuitive wisdom. This clarity can often reveal creative solutions.
5. Seek inspiration from diverse sources: Expose yourself to new experiences, perspectives, and disciplines. Cross-pollination of ideas from disparate realms can spark innovative problem-solving insights.
6. Remember to breathe and stay calm. Even when the problem is giving you anxiety, take a deep breath. You will be able to think of a solution. Alternatively, find someone who can help you, too. This is part of a problem-solving and open mindset—not being a drama queen but rather being part of the solution.

By embracing these practices and nurturing your innate creative genius, you'll unlock your artistic potential and cultivate a powerful problem-solving mindset that can help you navigate life's challenges with greater confidence, resilience, and creative ingenuity.

Remembering Our Mortality and Seizing the Present

In pursuing a creative awakening, it is essential to acknowledge the brevity of life. This concept resonates deeply with the stoic philosophy of memento mori, which urges us to remember that death is inevitable. By embracing our mortality, we can find a newfound appreciation for the present moment and harness our creative potential without delay. The notion of memento mori is a poignant reminder that life is short. We often become ensnared in the mundane routines dictated by societal expectations, postponing our artistic aspirations until some distant future. We believe creativity should be reserved for retirement or when we have ticked off all the boxes on society's checklist. However, this mindset stifles our imaginative spirit and robs us of experiencing true fulfillment in our creative endeavors. Imagine an artist who spends their entire life working tirelessly in a job they despise, longing for retirement when they can finally dedicate themselves fully to their artistic passions. They convince themselves that they must follow this prescribed path because it is what society deems responsible and practical. Yet, in doing so, they deny themselves the opportunity to nurture their soul through creativity during their prime years. The stoics would argue vehemently against such complacency. They advocate for living each day as if it were your last - not in a reckless manner but with an acute awareness of your limited time on Earth. By acknowledging death's inevitability, we are prompted to seize every moment and make conscious choices aligned with our deepest desires. Incorporating memento mori into our lives allows us to break free from societal shackles and embrace authenticity wholeheartedly. It compels us to question whether we are truly living or merely existing within predetermined boundaries set by others. Creativity becomes essential for self-expression and personal growth rather than just a hobby or pastime relegated to the sidelines. So, how can we infuse this philosophy into our creative journey? Firstly, it requires a shift in mindset. We must release ourselves from the illusion that creativity is only permissible under specific circumstances. There is no perfect time or age to embark on a creative endeavor; we only have the present moment. Secondly, it demands courage and resilience. Pursuing a creative path may not always align with societal expectations or guarantee financial stability. However, when we confront our mortality and recognize the fleeting nature of life, these concerns pale in comparison to the fulfillment gained from pursuing our passions. Thirdly, memento mori teaches us to detach ourselves from external validation and focus instead on the intrinsic value of our artistic pursuits. The true purpose of creativity lies within its ability to nourish our souls and provide an outlet for self-expression rather than seeking approval or recognition from others. Lastly, embracing mortality invites us to explore new artistic avenues fearlessly. Rather than adhering strictly to conventional norms or societal standards, we are encouraged to experiment with different mediums, styles, and techniques. By embracing imperfection and taking risks in our creative expression, we unlock hidden depths within ourselves that may have otherwise remained dormant. Memento mori serves as a powerful catalyst for our creative awakening. By acknowledging the brevity of life and embracing our mortality wholeheartedly, we can break free from societal constraints and live authentically through artistry at any stage of life. Let us seize this moment - for there is no greater gift than immersing ourselves fully in the present while nurturing our souls through creativity. Remember: Life is short; let us create without delay!

Reflections and Gratitude

The transformative power of embracing creativity is a journey that cannot be measured in mere words. It is a journey that takes one from the confines of a monotonous and stressful existence to a life filled with passion, fulfillment, and purpose. This journey began when I made the bold decision to leave behind my life as a practicing attorney and embark on a path of artistic exploration. Little did I know that this leap of faith would lead to a creative awakening that would forever change the course of my life. Looking back on this transformative journey, I am filled with awe and wonder. Adopting creativity has allowed me to shed the shackles of a 9-5 lifestyle and step into a world where my true passions and talents can flourish. No longer bound by the constraints of a rigid schedule and the pressures of a demanding profession, I have found freedom in creating art. But this journey is not just about personal transformation. It is also about the power of art to touch the lives of others. As I reflect on art's impact on my life, I am grateful for the many artists who have mentored me indirectly through their books, videos, paintings, and supportive messages. Their guidance and inspiration have been instrumental in shaping my creative journey, and I am forever grateful for their contributions. In addition to the artists who have influenced me, I am also grateful for the unwavering support of my family. Their belief in my abilities and their encouragement to take the risk of starting a new career as an artist has been invaluable. Without their support, I may have never had the courage to pursue my passion and embark on this transformative journey. One message stands out as I reflect on the key takeaways from my creative awakening: keep working. The path of creativity is not always easy, and there will inevitably be obstacles along the way. But it is through perseverance and dedication that true growth and transformation occur. So, to all those who are on their creative exploration, I urge you never to give up. Your work has significance, and your journey is worth pursuing. The creative awakening is a journey that transcends the boundaries of the ordinary and opens up a world of endless possibilities. It is a journey that transforms not only our own lives but the lives of those around us. As we continue to embrace creativity and share our experiences, let us do so with gratitude for the power of art and its profound impact on our lives. Let us continue to create, explore, and inspire others with our unique voices. And above all, let us never forget the transformative power of embracing our creativity.

About the Author

I want to thank you personally for reading this book. If you have reached this far, you are in the "one percent" category of people who finish what they started. Maybe we can shift that statistic a bit higher? Thanks to your self-discipline, you have achieved much. You will enjoy your life as a creatively awakened individual.

I also want to thank all those artists who study their craft with me. Whether you are a member of my Artist's Live Channel[1], own a course, or watch my YouTube videos[2]. You are also self-disciplined and no doubt experiencing growth in your art. My best wishes to you!

Further learning:

My courses on painting fundamentals: Learn to Paint with Impact[3].

Now, then, back into the third-person:

Author: Malcolm Dewey is a South African artist and writer. He paints in a contemporary Impressionist style and mostly paints landscapes and figures. He teaches painting in various mediums, including oils, acrylics, gouache, watercolor, and pastels. Malcolm sells his works to collectors all over the world, and his gallery can be viewed at www.malcolmdeweyfineart.com[4]

Connect with Malcolm on his website to join one of his free tutorials. Also Youtube/MalcolmDewey[5]

Finally, if you enjoyed this book, please give it a review on Amazon. Thank you!

---

1. https://malcolmdeweyfineart.newzenler.com/courses/artists-live-membership

2. https://www.youtube.com/MalcolmDewey

3. https://www.malcolmdeweyfineart.com/painting-course.html

4. https://www.malcolmdeweyfineart.com/painting-secrets.html

5. https://www.youtube.com/MalcolmDewey

Before you go

More books by Malcolm:

How to Loosen Up Your Painting

An Artist's Survival Guide

52 Weeks of Creativity

52 Weeks of Creative Mastery

Sell Your Art or Not?

Also by Malcolm Dewey

An Artist's Guide to Plein Air Painting
How to Loosen Up Your Painting
An Artist's Survival Guide
The Creative Living Book Bundle
The Art of Content Marketing
52 Weeks of Creative Living: Inspiration for Your Creative Soul
Your Artist's Voice
52 Weeks of Creative Mastery
Sell Your Art or Not?
The Creative Awakening